CHRISTIAN CIVILITY IN AN UNCIVIL WORLD

MITCH CARNELL, EDITOR

Smyth & Helwys Publishing, Inc.
6316 Peake Road
Macon, Georgia 31210-3960
1-800-747-3016
©2009 by Smyth & Helwys Publishing
All rights reserved.
Printed in the United States of America.

The paper used in this publication meets the minimum requirements of
American National Standard for Information Sciences—
Permanence of Paper for Printed Library Materials.
ANSI Z39.48–1984. (alk. paper)

Library of Congress Cataloging-in-Publication Data

Christian civility in an uncivil world / edited by Mitch Carnell.

p. cm.
Includes bibliographical references.
ISBN 978-1-57312-537-6 (pbk. : alk. paper)
1. Courtesy. 2. Christian life.
I. Carnell, C. Mitchell.
BV4647.C78C47 2009 241'.671—dc22 2009017014

Christian Civility IN AN UNCIVIL WORLD

MITCH CARNELL, ed.

To Carol, my wife, and to all of the other contributors, whose generous spirits have made this work a joy.

Words which do not give the light of Christ increase the darkness.

— *Mother Teresa*

Contents

Foreword, *Paul B. Raushenbush* 7

Preface, *Mitch Carnell* 11

Chapter 1: Bringing People of Faith Together 15
Jimmy R. Allen

Chapter 2: Good Manners for Public Christians 29
Richard J. Mouw

Chapter 3: What We Need Is More Maturity 47
Stacy F. Sauls

Chapter 4: Civility and the Common Good .63
John Gehring and Alexia Kelley

Chapter 5: Holy Conferencing 81
Sally Dyck

Chapter 6: The Minister as Friend 101
Thomas R. McKibbens

Chapter 7: Christian Civility on the Internet 117
Wade Burleson

Chapter 8: The Power of Words 127
Mitch Carnell

Contributors 145

Foreword

In a book about Christian civility, it is appropriate to begin with a confession. Recently I read an article featuring a pastor with whom I strongly disagreed. The more I read, the less I liked, and it was a *long* article. That pastor made statements about the nature of the gospel and society to which I took personal offense. Unfortunately, this happened right before I went to bed, and I spent an hour or so awake and fuming, wondering how this person could read the same Scriptures and see such a different Jesus than the one I call Lord.

The more I thought, the more I began to view a fellow Christian, whom I had never met and to whose beliefs I had been introduced third hand, as "the enemy." Like cement carelessly poured on a sidewalk, my thoughts hardened my heart into a stumbling block for my faith. Of course, my reaction isn't particularly unique or even surprising. Probably every reader of this book has experienced something similar—if we hadn't, the need for this book would not be so pressing.

Religion evokes intense responses because it plays an essential role in our lives. Our beliefs reflect who we are, what we care about, our purpose—what Tillich would call our "ultimate concerns." I serve as the Associate Dean of Religious Life and the Chapel at Princeton University. Much of my work involves encouraging interfaith dialogue between students of different religious traditions, including a group of thirty students called the Religious Life Council who have committed themselves to being part of a community of diverse faith traditions and beliefs (even atheists and agnostics) that acknowledges difference while maintaining respect and friendship.

This stretches the students, as Muslims and Jews, Hindus and Sikhs, Christians and Buddhists, articulate their disagreements on questions of the existence of God, how society should be structured, the relation between religion and international politics, and the nature of salvation. When speaking to someone from a different faith, we begin with the basic understanding that we will and should disagree, but we can sit down and have tea and talk together.

Interfaith dialogue is hard, but intrafaith dialogue can be harder. Every Christian claims Jesus as Savior and Lord, so essential questions of how we understand Jesus, his earthly ministry, the meaning of the crucifixion, and the nature of his call upon our lives (questions to which a non-Christian is largely indifferent) become the grounds of our essential debate and, literally, a matter of life and death. When we encounter a Christian who thinks and believes differently, we experience that difference as an attack on the principles upon which we have built our lives and as a betrayal to the faith. This feeling only increases when we add politics. In recent elections, both sides of the political aisle found inspiration and legitimization from Christian constituencies. Political debates often adopted theological rhetoric, and religious leaders adopted political strategies. The result has been a "winner take all" attitude with Christian groups being particularly brutal toward one another.

These battles are not new. I remember being disheartened in seminary by the contentious nature of our debates over Christian traditions and their social implications. A fellow student reminded me that, as evidenced in Paul's letters, Christians have disagreed since the days of the early church. The comment was meant to be comforting, and it is good to consider that our internal conflicts are not the result of any unique sinfulness of our time. But if we look at the history of our faith, we cannot gloss over the horrible violence committed by Christians, not only against people of other religions, but among ourselves. Thousands, maybe millions of people have died as the result of theological, social, or ecclesial differences. Thank God we do not appear to be anywhere near that point today, but our history looms as a warning. Civility, and more specifically Christian civility, serves as a safeguard against any threat of further violence or brutality. But more than simply being utilitarian, Christian civility should be adopted by every follower of Jesus as an important part of the spiritual discipline of our faith: not merely as one tool in our spiritual toolbox but as an integral part of what it means to be a Christian.

The word "civility" shares the same root as "citizen." Citizens of a common nation survive because they enter into the basic contract that they need one another, and that all individual citizens have a role to play so that they might enrich each other collectively. Laws are created that grant citizens individual rights balanced by mutual responsibilities to one another.

The locus of civility within the Christian life is the kingdom of God to which we are all granted citizenship through our faith. In God's kingdom, we are bound by the covenant of the two great commandments: that we love

God and love our neighbor as ourselves, even those whom we imagine to be our enemies. Civility in the kingdom of God demands a commitment to reconciliation that goes to the heart of the gospel.

Jesus stresses the importance of reconciliation in Matthew 5:23-24 when he instructs his followers not to come to the altar if we are in a dispute with one of our sisters or brothers. In this age of the Internet in which anonymous vitriol and cruelty is as convenient as a click of the keyboard, Jesus' specific demand that we approach the one with whom we have a disagreement face to face offers a profound correction. Just like the interfaith engagement of my students at Princeton, personal interaction forces us to recognize the humanity in the person whom otherwise we might easily demonize or dismiss. The more we know about a person, the more we appreciate their vulnerabilities, their aspirations, and the reasons for their convictions. Hopefully we might ultimately acknowledge that God is working in her or his life as well as in our own.

The advantage of being authentically engaged with people whose beliefs differ from our own is that it serves as a safeguard against idolizing our personal ideology. If we spend time only with people who nod affirmatively, we risk the casual merging of our own truth with the gospel truth and the subsuming of the Way of Jesus to our own way. When we become adherents of our own certitude, our faith can calcify and stagnate. Christian civility requires humility, a somewhat underemphasized virtue among Christian leaders. Yet our commitment to "walk humbly with our God," as Micah 6:8 requires, gives space for us to learn and grow from God and from our Christian brothers and sisters.

Christian civility does not mean that we won't disagree. There is a difference between incivility and disagreement. Incivility breaks down communication and ruptures God's kingdom, but disagreement between Christians is inevitable, and even productive. One example is the disagreement between Christian leaders around the Civil Rights Movement in America. Many Christians encouraged Martin Luther King, Jr., to temper his demands, to slow down his movement, and not to create so much tension or disagreement. King responded in his now famous Letter from Birmingham City Jail, "But I must confess that I am not afraid of the word tension. I have earnestly worked and preached against violent tension, but there is a type of constructive nonviolent tension that is necessary for growth." Like MLK, Jr., we all benefit from clarity about where we stand. A call for civility is not a call for lack of conviction; rather, it is about remaining engaged with those with whom we disagree in the hopes that we might somehow continue to move forward together, forging new consensus as we go. The American civil rights movement is one example of civil tension that led Christians to a more authentic faith.

Christians will continue to experience tension with each other until we all agree on everything or Jesus comes again—and I am betting on Jesus. Therefore, the call for civility begins today and with each one of us. Christian civility doesn't work if it is reduced to my pointing the finger at someone else and telling him or her to be more civil. While I still disagree with the pastor of my earlier confession, instead of only pointing out the speck in his eye I should start by paying more attention to the log in my own. Perhaps then, when we can see each other more clearly, we will be granted the vision to build bridges into the future.

In our efforts toward greater Christian civility, we need help and encouragement. That is why this book is such a blessing. The contributors represent a wide range of theological and political perspectives, yet each is committed to the practice of Christian civility and offers concrete examples of how it is done. Hopefully the insight within these pages will create a groundswell among Christians so that civility might be a sign by which one recognizes a Christian in this world, and through our word and deed greater glory might be given to our Lord Jesus.

Paul B. Raushenbush
Princeton University, 2009

Preface

In 2005 I volunteered to help students with their writing skills at the inner-city middle school where my wife was teaching. As I met with these students and teachers, I was deeply troubled about their pervasive negativity and hopelessness. Someone had to do something. I wrote a little booklet titled *Say Something Nice; Be a Lifter*, which I wanted to give to the students. I was totally unsuccessful with the public and private schools; however, I was remarkably successful with the administration and staff of the city of North Charleston and with the neighborhood organization presidents of the city of Charleston.

Mayor Keith Summey of North Charleston declared June 1, 2006, as the first Say Something Nice Day. He did the same in 2007 and was joined by Mayor Joe Riley of Charleston. During this same period, disrespect and unchristian discourse continued to escalate in the Christian community. There was a great need to temper this rhetoric. It was destroying the Christian witness and message. Dr. Frank Page, the new president of the Southern Baptist Convention, was elected partly because he promised to be more conciliatory in his relations with those who did not share his point of view. The presiding bishop of the Episcopal Church attempted the same approach. I proposed to the First Baptist Church of Charleston, the oldest Baptist church in the South, that we sponsor Say Something Nice Sunday and invite other denominations and churches to join us. First Baptist Church agreed, and the pastor, the Reverend Marshall Blalock, was highly supportive. The Charleston Baptist Association joined in the effort, as did the Charleston Atlantic Presbytery, the Cooperative Baptist Fellowship, and many other churches throughout South Carolina.

I posted an article on the Christian News Wire about our efforts. After it was published, the unexpected happened. Various fundamentalists groups and individuals attacked me, First Baptist Church, and Rev. Blalock for watering down the gospel. I received dozens of e-mails telling me that Christians were not to be nice to non-Christians.

About this time, Russell Dilday, fired president of Southwestern Baptist Seminary, published *Higher Ground*, and Brian Kaylor released *For God's*

Sake, Shut Up! Both books attacked the same issue of uncontrolled speech. I discovered Richard Mouw's book *Uncommon Decency*, which is absolutely marvelous. All of these were additional fuel to my motivation, which had already been greatly influenced by Quentin Schultze's *Communicating for Life.*[1]

My wife, Carol, and I have been captivated by the Chautauqua Institution's program for many years. Our experiences at Chautauqua have taught us that respectful Christian dialogue is possible. We have heard speakers and preachers representing many points of view. We have attended joint services with Muslims and Jews. We have shared in an ecumenical Communion service. We have been blessed by the opportunity to share give-and-take sessions. We have been strengthened in our faith by these experiences. It is safe to say that we cannot get enough of these experiences that stretch our understanding and enlarge our souls. Of course, there are always a few who are not open to new or different ideas, but these are greatly outnumbered by those who participate in order to consider thoughtfully what is offered before either accepting or rejecting it.

It is difficult to pinpoint where widespread lack of civility started in the church. The Bible cites many examples of rancor and disagreements in the early churches. Perhaps they have always existed, but the twenty-four-hour hunger of the mass media has made such lack of civility more obvious. It was certainly there when I was a small boy growing up in a small mill village in South Carolina. It took years for me to reject the ignorance about the Roman Catholic Church that characterized so many comments I heard from well-meaning but uninformed Protestant ministers. I never bought into the prejudice toward Jews simply because I was well acquainted with a wonderful Jewish family. I knew them to be generous and kind people. I was always distressed when various churches set out on a campaign to convert this family.

In more recent times, President Ronald Reagan melded the Religious Right into the foundation of the Republican Party. President Bill Clinton provided them with all the ammunition they needed to launch the nasty campaign against him and all democrats that continues to this day. Pat Robertson and Jerry Falwell added their shrill voices of hate and disrespect to the mix. Those who disagreed or raised even a hint of protest were accused of not believing the Bible. The election of Bishop Gene Robinson, an openly gay priest, turned the Episcopal Church upside down and inside out. It assured everyone both within and outside the Episcopal Church that the forces of evil were advancing. Dr. Albert Mohler, president of the Southern Baptist Seminary, quickly joined the fray with attacks on the gay community.

A remarkable conference took place at First Baptist Church of Charleston on August 1, 2, and 3, 2007. Historians from all branches of the Baptist tradition met to discuss their heritage. Primitive, Seventh Day, American, National, General, Cooperative, Conservative, and Southern Baptists historians all met together. It was an outstanding meeting that went smoothly. The singing of traditional hymns and spirituals was so amazing that several speakers commented that perhaps we should stop talking and just sing. At the pre-conference, there was an agreement not to use the church's magnificent pipe organ, but by the end of the conference everyone's minds had changed. How can we sit in the presence of this great organ and not hear it? If all of these factions of Baptist life can meet together, perhaps there is hope for real dialogue.

Over the last twelve years, I have met with a wonderful group of pastors. For a time we met monthly, but now, because of the meeting's importance to us, we meet weekly. Every person in the group is a minister or retired minister except me. All of them were at one time Southern Baptists. All of them are now in separate denominations except me. The discussions are far reaching. Of course, not all of the discussions are serious. We share many preacher jokes. From time to time, we invite visitors to come and talk about his or her point of view or particular work. These have included the religion editor of the local newspaper, an orthodox priest, the director of a statewide counseling program, a retired public relations officer from the Nuclear Regulatory Commission, a columnist, visiting ministers from out of town, and local clergy.

For as long as I can remember, I have been interested in what the Bible has to say about communication and how we relate to one another. The story of the Tower of Babel captured my imagination. Pentecost reversed the effects of the Tower of Babel. In the Babel account, language was confused and made divisive in order to sabotage a ridiculous enterprise. In our dealings with one another, in individual churches, denominations, and between denominations, our language is still divisive and destructive. With many it is as if Pentecost never happened. Pentecost is a great homecoming where people from all nations heard and understood in their own languages. *Understood* is the key word. We are to strive for understanding. We are all different, but we are all part of one body.

The thrust of this book is to explore ways for people of faith to talk to and about each other in a way that glorifies God and advances God's kingdom. It is possible for Christians to retain their differences and yet unite in respect for each other. It is possible to love one another and at the same time retain our individual beliefs. The contributors represent some of the most brilliant minds and biggest hearts in the Christian faith. Dr. Jimmy Allen, whom I have long admired, gave me thumbs up. Tom McKibbens provided high enthusiasm. Wade Burleson attracted my attention with his Internet blog. My brother-in law, Joe Gilliland, pointed me to Bishop Stacy Sauls, who is a fellow Furman graduate. Bishop Sally Dyck intrigued me with the idea of holy conferencing. I heard Dr. Paul Raushenbush at Chautauqua and knew that I had to enlist his help. Paul sent me to Alexia Kelley and John Gehring. Carol, my wife, has supported the project every step of the way. Without her help and gentle persuasion, there would be no book. I receive tremendous support and encouragement from the great congregation and staff at First Baptist Church. Leslie Andres, our editor at Smyth &Helwys, provided great help and encouragement.

I have sought God's guidance in carrying out this project. I truly believe that God planted the idea in my mind that such a book was needed. The enthusiastic response from the other contributors provided further evidence. There was no burning bush, just a constant tugging that gave way to excitement. Every day brings new evidence that there is a pressing need for Christians to model Christ in our relationships with each other and with the nonbelieving world. We are each God's creation, and we cannot love God and disrespect or denigrate one another. My prayer is that you will read this book in the spirit in which it was written. I am a layperson; therefore, I proceeded with that perspective. I believe that we can talk together, listen to each other, change the Christian dialogue, and thus change our world. We know from the start that we will not agree on all of the hot-button issues, but we also know in the depth of our beings that we serve the same God and that we are all seekers.

"Come let us reason together" (Isa 1:18).

Mitch Carnell
Charleston, South Carolina

Note

1. Dilday and Kaylor, both Macon GA: Smyth & Helwys Publishing, 2007; Mouw, Downers Grove IL: Intervarsity Press, 1992; Schultze, Grand Rapids MI: Baker Books, 2000.

Chapter 1

Bringing People of Faith Together

Jimmy R. Allen,
Coordinator of the New Baptist Covenant

The idea of bringing grassroots people of faith together is finding its day. Uniting Christian groups into common endeavors is not a new concept. Church councils, ecumenical structures, and denominational groups dot the landscape of Christian history. The thing that is new is a shift to grassroots relationships.

Civility Is Not Enough

In the Christian community, our relationships should be more than civil. They should reach toward brotherhood and mutual concerns and actions. Civility is not mere politeness. It is not a matter of getting people to say "excuse me, please" while stabbing each other in the back. It is not a matter of silencing people or asking them to roll over and play dead while their interests or questions are ignored in the decision-making process. It is not avoiding important issues simply because they are difficult to address.

Civility has moved from a Webster definition of merely being a part of the body politic into a mode of relating to each other with respect. In the words of the co-founder of the Johns Hopkins Civility Project, Dr. P. M. Forni, "Civility is linked to the Latin word 'civitas' which meant 'city' and 'community.' Thus, civility implies a larger social concern. When we are civil, we are members in good standing of a community, we are good neighbors and good citizens. Whether we look at the core of manners or at that of civility we discern not only pleasant form but ethical substance as well."[1] Conflict resolution and the search for civility in human relationships have become a matter of urgent concern in recent days. This concern has always been with us, but in a crowded world headed for new degrees of globalization, it is now critical. One sign of this is that a Google search reveals more than three and a half million references to the subject!

The Baptist Movement: A Case Study in Recovering Civility

The Baptist movement in America provides a case study of the challenges of civility and unity. Baptists are the largest of the Free Church denominations and are characterized by adult baptism and encouraging religious freedom and separation of church and state. It is estimated that there are thirty-nine million baptized believers in the Baptist movement in North America. The Baptist movement offers an excellent case study for recovering civility because its nature emphasizes freedom of decision making both individually and congregationally; therefore, attitudes become a major factor in relationships.

Bringing People of Faith Together

The Baptist movement emerged four hundred years ago as a rejection of the British Empire's efforts to adopt a universal Book of Common Prayer as it sought to solidify its state-sponsored separation from the Roman Catholic Church. John Smyth (1570–1612) and Thomas Helwys (1550–1616) addressed the king with a letter rejecting the right of the state to make such decisions. Helwys died in Newgate Prison. Smyth died in Holland. While they disagreed and separated in their ministry, the two were joined in their rejection of the right of the state to govern religion. In the Colonies, Roger Williams, persecuted for his similar beliefs, had to flee the persecution of the Pilgrims and eventually founded Rhode Island. It became the first place in the world to declare that religious freedom was a basic right of every citizen. There the first Baptist church in America was founded.

Early Baptists were involved in constant controversy. Their belief in the priesthood of the believer and the necessity of a voluntary response to God, the authority of the Scripture, and the responsibility of each believer to interpret it under the leadership of the Holy Spirit cut against the grain of the establishment. They were jailed or driven out of many places. However, largely through their efforts, the first amendment to the U.S. Constitution, guaranteeing religious liberty through separation of church and state, was adopted. These Baptists were uniquely equipped for the expanding frontier. They believed their preachers were called of God rather than appointed by church hierarchies. Therefore, their lay preachers were ordained by local congregations and set free to preach. They started training schools for those who were already called and doing their ministries. Often they walked to their places of preaching, and therefore pastors visited their churches for occasional services, while laypeople carried out the main ministry. They were often opinionated and fractious in their debates about the meaning of the Bible but united in believing that the Bible was the sole authority for faith and practice. The ministries for orphaned children, hospitals, schools, and mission endeavors came as a grassroots response to obvious needs. The story of meeting those needs is the story of the growing of a great denomination of Christians in this country.

Divisive Factors in the Baptist Movement

The story, however, is also to recount some of the divisive factors in the North American Baptist experience that must be confronted in the process of recovery of effectiveness in the kingdom of God.

Racism

Racism and slavery produced the darkest chapter in the history of the Baptist movement. As the importation of slave labor rose in the cotton/tobacco area of the South, the Baptist challenge was overwhelming and complicated. On the one hand, the practice of slavery brought many people from Africa. Baptist believers felt a responsibility for their religious needs to be met. They started allowing African Americans in balconies and other sections during their worship services. Many slaves became baptized believers under that system of separation. Gifted orators evolved in the Black congregations, and marvelous music reflected their tribal histories as it came out in gospel singing. More than ten million Baptist believers in our day are affiliated with the National Baptist Convention (the name chosen for predominately African-American Baptist churches).

On the other hand, these people were hard pressed to find a biblical defense of slavery. Thus, a white supremacy interpretation of the Scripture developed. It took the form of justifying slavery and calling for fair treatment of slaves within the system. Racial segregation has fragmented the Baptist movement beyond description.

It is ironic that so many of the major voices against racism have come from African-American Baptists who fashioned their future in tune with the teachings of the gospel. The division of our nation between North and South over the slavery issue also divided the Anglo Baptist fellowships. The

Northern Baptist Convention (now American Baptist Churches/USA) separated when the Southern Baptist Convention formed over the issue of abolition of slavery. While racism knows no geographic boundaries, the separation of fellowships has created chasms that must be bridged if the Baptist movement is to be effective.

The barriers built by racism have been a serious challenge to the claims of the gospel to make God's people one. The sad truth is that the most segregated hour in our nation's experience remains the eleven o'clock Sunday worship hour. No amount of glib explanations can cover the fact that racism seeps unconsciously into our beings and is a denial of the essentials of our faith.

Fundamentalism

One of the divisive elements in the Baptist movement has been the presence of fundamentalism. All religions are subject to the radical voices of extremism. Our world is being torn apart these days by the absence of civility in religious behavior. For the Baptist movement, fundamentalism and conservative resurgences have periodically asserted themselves.

Fundamentalism has a way of forming around powerful personalities. It thrives on conflict. It creates patterns of conformity around wedge issues that become shibboleth tests of faith and fidelity. It produces an atmosphere of divisiveness.

In the 1930s, one of the outstanding voices of fundamentalism came out of the Southwest. He was J. Frank Norris from First Baptist Church of Ft. Worth, Texas. After some time in which he struggled to lead Texas Baptists, he withdrew and created his own convention. Like more current fundamentalists, he constantly attacked others, focusing particularly on George W. Truett, of First Baptist Church, Dallas, and J. M. Dawson, who became the national director of the Baptist Joint Committee on Public Affairs. Norris organized his own seminary in opposition to Southwestern Baptist Theological Seminary in his hometown. He also started a church in Detroit, Michigan, and flew there to preach every other Sunday.

In 1945 the Baptist General Convention of Texas (BGCT) had its annual session in the First Baptist Church of Amarillo, Texas. As a college sophomore and student pastor, I accompanied my parents to the convention. The major speaker for the meeting was Dr. Louie D. Newton, pastor of Druid Hills Baptist Church in Atlanta and president of the Baptist World Alliance. As president of the BWA, he had gone on a trip around the world to visit with Baptist churches and leaders. On the trip, he had an audience with the Pope in Rome and visited with Joseph Stalin in Moscow. J. Frank Norris had attacked Newton as being soft on Communism and Catholicism (both his constant targets). Dr. Norris was ill and could not come to Amarillo for the convention, so he sent his associate, Dr. Frazier, who ran his seminary. Frazier secured a sound truck and drove around the church building where the convention met, blaring the message that Newton was a Communist and urging the people not to go in to hear him. The police forced the truck to operate a block away, but the volume was high enough to carry the message.

On the day Dr. Newton spoke, Dr. Frazier came to the meeting and sat several rows back on the stage left. I happened to be seated three pews behind him. There was word that he planned to disrupt the meeting. Dr. Wallace Bassett, pastor of the Cliff Temple Baptist Church in Dallas and former pastor of the Amarillo church, was presiding as president of the BGCT. He arranged for three large and athletic young pastors to sit by and behind Frazier. When Newton was introduced, all was quiet. As he started to speak, Frazier jumped up shouting that Newton was a Communist. The three young pastors picked up Frazier and carried him bodily out of the meeting, still shouting. I sat enthralled by the drama. Dr. Newton was a brilliant, folksy, Southern gentleman. He was an eloquent speaker. However, this day was one in which he wanted to be careful with his words, so he read from a manuscript. It was not his style, and he began to drone on with his message. The young preachers had returned from their task of ejection. As I sat there, I heard Fred Swank lean over and, in a stage whisper, say to Wayland Boyd, who had helped him carry out Frazier, "I think we carried out the wrong man!"

In typical Fundamentalist pattern, J. Frank Norris created a competing fellowship of churches. These faded from the scene with his death, but his tribe has increased in our current experience.

Fundamentalism is not so much a system of literalist interpretations of the Bible as it is a mindset. All religions have their elements of fundamentalism. It is typical of fundamentalist to work in harmony with others on various matters of common concern so long as the fundamentalists wield less than fifty percent of the power. Once they gain fifty-one percent, fundamentalists reject and remove those who oppose their point of view.

This narrow interpretation of the gospel has much of its negative impact because many leaders are unwilling to challenge it. Current Baptists try to avoid attacks by vying with each other about how conservative their interpretations of the Bible could be.

The relationship is complicated in recent years by the marriage of religious conservatism and right-wing politics. Later experiences of Baptists with other voices, including a number of television evangelists, have proven that the search for both political and denominational power can be successful by preying on the fears of people of faith. Civility disappears when these fears are stoked.

Regionalism

Religious movements tend to take on the perspectives and cultural values of their regions, and this can create real division among different regions. Urbanization, globalization, communication by Internet, and other factors are altering the patterns of human relationships. However, many of us are still under the powerful influence of the customs and values of our communities. We must deal with differences in perspective.

Geographical differences are real differences. The same factors that affect us in our other behaviors affect our religious practice. Texans will be Texans. New Yorkers will be New Yorkers. Southerners will be Southerners. Despite the communications revolution and the ease of travel, Americans born today are actually more likely to reside near their places of birth than those who lived in the nineteenth century. Part of this is due to our aging population, because older people are far less likely to move than those under thirty.

The love of God establishes a relationship in which brotherhood exists and trust develops. The patterns of our lives have to accommodate those who do not fit them. This can be an enriching experience. However, it is a challenge to reach across the chasms to establish levels of trust and oneness.

Affluence and Poverty

The Baptist movement is also a case study because of the chasms that exist in our faith groups between the affluent and the poor. The color of our problem is not just black and white; it is also green. The Baptist movement started, as did many others, among the common people. Local churches ordained preachers in response to their showing evidence of a call from God. No hierarchal system controlled the process. Churches voluntarily related to each other in associations. Most of the pastors were bi-vocational. While persons of educational achievement and skills were involved and urged further training of those responding to the call, the training was not a requirement for ordination.

The emphasis on individual responsibility and the opportunities of our emerging society made the upward movement of our economic position inevitable. We became affluent and began to reflect it as we pondered the "undeserving poor" as a problem instead of an opportunity to serve. Like many other faith groups, we have to be reminded that the poor "heard Christ gladly."

The story, however, is also of dealing with controversies in a fair and reasonable manner. Today the divisions and differences among us are usually couched in the "language of Zion." We do not easily admit that we are divided by racism, localism, class attitudes, or regional differences. We choose to word our differences as doctrinal and scriptural interpretations. We talk of whether or not our opponents believe the Bible. We argue over whether women should be pastors (now the issue is senior pastors). We talk of whether gays or lesbians should be allowed to have equal civil rights in their commitments to each other. We speak of whether a fetus has all the rights of a baby. We talk about whether God really loves the entire world or just those He has already chosen to be His. We talk about end times and the implication of the earth's being scorched and embattled rather than mankind's responsibility to "tend the garden" with which God has entrusted us.

The New Baptist Covenant Celebration

The high-water mark of a recovery of civility among Baptists in the American experience came in Atlanta, Georgia, in January 2008 with the Celebration of the New Baptist Covenant. The gathering represented the 22-million majority of Baptists in North America. More than 15,000 people from all racial, regional, doctrinal, and economic groups came together around the common ground of the Luke 4 mandate: "The Spirit of the Lord is upon me, because he hath anointed me to preach the gospel to the poor; he hath sent me to heal the brokenhearted, to preach deliverance to the captives, and recovering of sight to the blind, to set at liberty them that are bruised, to preach the acceptable year of the Lord" (vv. 18-19). Citing this command of Jesus, the group represented the majority of Baptists in the United States of America. They were from more than thirty Baptist organizations.

The challenge was (and still is) how to bring a level of civility and common commitment within such diverse groups in the name of our commitment to Christ. The story of the New Baptist Covenant Celebration reveals several essential ingredients for achieving civility and discovering common ground for sharing our service to our Lord. The aim of the initial meeting was to gather grassroots believers who want to live out the practical implications of their faith in order to find out how they can do it better and together.

The Content of the Covenant

We Baptists of North America covenant together to:
• Create an authentic and prophetic Baptist voice for these complex times,
• Emphasize traditional Baptist values, including sharing the gospel of Jesus Christ and its implications for public and private morality, and
• Promote peace with justice, feed the hungry, clothe the naked, shelter the homeless, care for the sick and marginalized, welcome the strangers among us, and promote religious liberty and respect for religious diversity.[2]

The Birth of the Covenant

Creative ideas often emerge from unlikely places. In the case of the New Baptist Covenant, the idea emerged from a conversation between two Baptist laymen who occupied strategic positions of responsibility. They were meeting for the first time. It was early spring 2006. President Jimmy Carter, deacon and Sunday school teacher at Plains, Georgia, was visited at the Carter Center by Bill Underwood, attorney and deacon recently moving from Baylor University in Waco, Texas, to serve as president of Mercer University in Macon, Georgia. As they chatted about the state of Baptists with their battles over control of Southern Baptist Convention institutions, diminishing effectiveness in mission, token efforts for racial reconciliation, and vast potential for impact, the idea emerged that leaders from the various conventions who were still in touch with each other following the withdrawal of the largest single convention from the Baptist World Alliance be invited for a discussion of the future.[3]

The goal was that the meeting be inclusive, bring no preconceived plan, and discover possible responses to the challenge of bringing a level of civility and common commitment within such diverse groups. No official structures of denominations were asked to send representation. Instead, persons were invited across various denominational structures. The process was brainstormed all along. The meeting was conducted at the Carter Center, a site noted for initiatives in meeting human rights and human needs under the impetus of President Carter's foundation. While President Carter had made several attempts to bring harmony or at least civility by meeting with Convention leaders before, those encounters were less than successful. This time the meeting would be a one-time effort to explore possibilities among a cross section of leaders invited from all Baptist entities.

The decision was to make the centerpiece of the gathering the sharing of "best practices" in showing the love of Christ to the marginalized and hurting people of the world. Baptists are blessed with many outstanding leaders. The plenary sessions featured several of them. The special-interest sections allowed people to choose to hear from others about practical ways of ministry as well as to hear prophetic preachers proclaiming the truth. Time was provided for conversation among those facing particular challenges. They could follow up with each other for future communication and joint efforts. Participants described the event as an experience of the Spirit of the Lord among them as they were led to discover brothers and sisters in faith separated by long-standing barriers but still ministering and meeting the same challenges in their neighborhoods. They determined to reach across the historic and attitudinal barriers that divided them and find ways to join in common causes.

Look for and Build on Previous Experiences of Working Together

These laymen decided to invite the members of the Baptist World Alliance's North American Baptist Fellowship as participants. This fellowship included representatives from each of the participating national conventions and met regularly as part of the Alliance's activities. It had members from most Baptist groups in the United States and Canada. For some time, they had gathered with the opportunity for fellowship and exchanging of views. Underfunded, they hoped for an opportunity to expand their activities.

The presidents of the five National Baptist Conventions (predominantly African-American) were included in the invitations. Three years before this time, at the suggestion of William Shaw, president of the National Baptist Convention Inc., the largest of these conventions, all five of them moved their midwinter meeting to a central place in order to work more effectively. That meeting was held at Opryland Convention Center in Nashville, Tennessee. It created a significant prelude for the emerging New Baptist Covenant Celebration. A vital part of the success of the celebration was the decision by each convention to join in the midwinter sessions of their own groups prior to the beginning of the celebration.

Another significant event was a decision two years earlier by the American Baptist Churches/USA and the Cooperative Baptist Fellowship to have a simultaneous annual gathering in Washington, D.C., with a closing unified service. The former Northern Baptist Convention and the CBF, which moved out of the Southern Baptist Convention, were reaching out to each other. Hurricane Katrina provided opportunities for several of these groups to integrate their disaster-relief efforts. They had become aware of each other and acquainted in the common effort to assist people in the spirit of the New Baptist Covenant before the covenant was even formed.

Included in the group steering the preparation for the celebration were informal groups such as the organization of laypeople called Mainstream Baptists. Some 70,000 persons on their mailing list were contacted with the information about the celebration. Persons involved in the Baptist press network were invited and assisted in communicating about the activities taking place in this unity-themed meeting. Representatives of financial institutions such as the Ministers and Missionaries Benefit Board of the American Baptist Convention participated in the planning and presentations at the sessions. Leaders of educational institutions, including a number of college and seminary presidents, participated from the inception of the planning. Women's groups in each of the conventions were involved. Laymen involved in such efforts as disaster-relief teams, leaders in hands-on poverty ministries, publishing houses, and benevolence ministries both domestically and internationally were included.

Choose to Deal with the Real Challenges of Applying the Principles of Christ to Life

We will never discover what we have in common across the chasms that separate us if we simply try to be polite and affirming of each other. Discovering our differences and trying to explain them will bring some understanding but will not change relationships. We do more by working together on common challenges, developing trust in each other, and finding ways to meet the needs of others than we can do with polite conversations. Having joint worship services is a healthy step, but we must be able to answer the crucial "So what?" questions. Are we doing something to bring change to hurting people? That is an urgent issue. We need to accept that our goal is to achieve not *uniformity* but *unity*. Unity is achieved under fire as we stand fast in our caring actions. The Luke 4 mandate serves well to keep our path directed toward the marginalized and hurting of our world.

Out of the discussions during planning sessions, we decided the special interest session schedule would focus on best practices. This way, we were able to call on all our participants to share insights from real experience. Breaking the cycles of poverty, engaging the criminal justice system, getting along with those of other faiths, dealing with sexual exploitation, reaching out to the sick, peacemaking, welcoming strangers in the issues of immigration, dealing with the HIV/AIDS pandemic, providing relief from disasters, and defining and claiming our religious freedom move along the same common ground of need as sharing our faith and growing our spiritual disciplines. For example, a luncheon in which Nobel Prize winner and former vice president Al Gore made a faith-based presentation about his book *Inconvenient Truth* opened the door for responders to join in the task of trusteeship of the garden of earth.[4]

Include Everyone Possible and Listen Carefully

One of the keys to bringing disparate elements of the faith community together effectively is the determination to include everyone possible as early as possible and to listen carefully to their contributions. People who could strengthen our efforts sometimes are overlooked. We need to hear from those who are deeply involved in the areas of our efforts. We need to learn of successes and of failures. We often learn more from what failed so we can avoid repeating mistakes. We need to listen to success with an ear toward applying the answers to our own needs. We need to be patient in determining if we are hearing what is being communicated. Then we need to act on what we have heard.

Enlist and Work with the Young

The decision to offer scholarships to some interns in preparing for the celebration was the means of getting in touch with and staying in touch with youth groups and college and seminary students. In any effort of bringing faith groups together, a key element is the infusion of youthful energy. Youth need the experience and we need the connection with the future. The presence of scores of students taking notes for the credit they earned in the meeting made a significant impact. The formation of young Baptist business people into a fellowship as well as the theological fellowship extended the impact of the meeting itself. Social networking is a lively reality with the young in this age of communication. This group is a great asset in seeking to establish relationships in the New Baptist Covenant movement.

Deal with Controversy and Opposition

Controversy has been part of the gene pool of the Baptist movement. The priesthood of the believer concept means that each believer comes to the Scripture with the promise that the Spirit will guide him or her into all truth. Creeds are rejected, though descriptions of the faith and message are created and accepted. Room for differences is deliberately provided. Victimized and vilified by the authorities of established hierarchies, early Baptists became accustomed to defending their views. When they could not find agreement, they separated into other congregations. Churches split easily and new associations were formed. The common cause of missions to take the message to others, evangelism to share the good news with the searchers, and ministry to the orphaned and needy united them by centrifugal force.

Critics will always find ways to discredit efforts to bring people together with civility and common endeavors. In the case of the New Baptist Covenant, one criticism was centered in apprehension that we were gathered for political purposes. The fact that our co-chair and convener of the planning meeting was President Carter and that a number of leaders enlisted to speak to issues were Baptists who had held high public office as democrats added fuel to that flame. We were caught in the usually long presidential campaigns. The issues of the Luke 4 mandate call for actions within the community and nation that include political leadership. Balancing the Baptist leaders who could address the issues between political parties was complex. However, we were able to secure a broad section of leadership not only from the world of politics but also from the world of medicine, sports, education, criminal justice, finance, human rights, missions, evangelism, family issues, global warming, and trusteeship of the earth.

There was apprehension from some that this was a major new effort to establish a convention or a super convention. This idea was rejected from the first. No new structure was envisioned or enabled. We hoped and prayed that the meeting would reflect a movement at the grass roots toward more effective cooperation. In addition, the basic principle was announced from the beginning that there be no negative words about any group of Baptists. We sought to find positive ways of working in the future rather than lament or make accusations about differences in the past.

Conclusions

The decision to urge celebrants to go home and find ways to implement the New Baptist Covenant is now revealing a stirring of movement at the grassroots level. Regional celebrations of the New Baptist Covenant have emerged in 2009 and 2010. With no promotional mechanism or official office, they are keeping in touch with each other through e-mail and websites. The T. B.

Maston Foundation for Christian Ethics has assumed the task of h
support a single-person office of coordinator for the New Baptist Cov
as the movement emerges. The first regional celebration was planne
Birmingham, Alabama. It was held on the anniversary of the original c
bration, January 30, at the 19th Avenue Baptist Church in Birminghan
There were two such celebrations in April 2009: one in Winston-Salem,
North Carolina, at Wake Forest University and another in Kansas City,
Missouri, under the banner of Crossing Borders. A fourth one will be in
Norman, Oklahoma's new Convention Center in August 2009. Plans for
2010 include celebrations in Chicago, Illinois; Los Angeles, California; and
New York City. In the triennial year, another national gathering is projected.
On their own response, two dozen New Baptist Covenant participants have
become presenters of the Faith Based Climate Control Challenge program
with a commitment to make at least ten presentations a year. The Young
Baptist Network is actively enlisting persons for the celebrations, participating in the Climate Control Challenge, and projecting a national gathering of
their own in 2010.

Meanwhile, word streams in of churches and Baptist groups crossing
previous barriers to work with each other in the fields the New Baptist
Covenant Celebration provided. Universities and seminaries are pressing the
causes of justice and especially the concerns about torture, hunger, and the
HIV/AIDS pandemic. Language groups and churches with multiracial fellowships are reminding us of the plight of those caught up in immigration
problems, and new programs of support are evolving.

Quo vadis? Where are you going? The question is vital, real, challenging,
and unanswerable. Only God knows. We will find out!

Notes

1. P. M. Forni, *Choosing Civility: The Twenty-five Rules of Considerate Conduct* (New York: St. Martin's, 2002); see also "Dr. Forni's Civility Web Site," http://krieger.jhu.edu/civility.

2. View the full statement at http://www.newbaptistcovenant.org/index.php?option=com_content&task=view&id=15&Itemid=37.

3. The Cooperative Baptist Fellowship (CBF) was formed by moderate Baptists after losing political leadership in the Southern Baptist Convention (SBC). When the Baptist World Alliance voted to accept CBF into their world fellowship, the SBC withdrew from the Alliance. The moderate point of view can be found in *The Struggle for the Soul of the SBC: Moderate Responses to the Fundamentalist Movement* by Walter Shurden (Macon GA: Mercer University Press, 1993). The fundamentalist point of view can be found in *A Hill on Which to Die* by Paul Pressler (Nashville: B&H Publishing Group, 1999).

4. Al Gore, *An Inconvenient Truth: The Crisis of Global Warming* (rev. ed.; New York: Viking, 2007).

Chapter 2

Good Manners for Public Christians

Richard J. Mouw,
President of Fuller Theological Seminary

A few years ago, I visited a political leader at his office in Washington, D.C. This is a person who gets good marks from the Religious Right for the stands that he takes—certainly better marks than I would be given. But he and I share the same basic Christian worldview, which means we can have good conversations together about matters of common interest.

The first time I visited this person, we talked about specific policy questions, but this time around he had a bigger topic on his mind. With a worried look on his face, he posed a question to me. "Give me an honest answer," he said. "From your perspective out there on the West Coast, how do we look here in Washington?"

"Okay," I said, "I will give you an honest answer. You folks don't look too good these days. Things are very polarized."

"Well," he said, "it's even worse than you probably realize. It's really discouraging. We used to be able to talk to each other in calm tones, even when we represent different perspectives—give-and-take and all that. But now it's all us versus them. We need a good dose of uncommon decency." When he said these last words he smiled, letting me know that he knew the title of one of my books. But the smile faded when he added, "And, you know, maybe we believers in public life need it more than anyone else."

Though we had this conversation a few years ago, the basic theme keeps getting repeated. Even as I write this, I have just returned from a meeting where a business leader visiting our campus asked me, "What is this seminary doing to help tone down the harsh rhetoric that we hear all the time these days, both in the church and the larger society? We need some teaching on good manners!"

That's what I want to talk about here: good manners. Not that I see myself as a "Miss Manners" type. She and the other folks who write advice columns give quite detailed advice to specific questions posed by real people. The advice I am going to give here is not detailed, and I am not responding (for the most part) to actual requests for advice. It is close to the truth to say that I am giving answers to questions I wish a lot of people *were* asking these days.

Convictions and Civility

That political leader referred to my book on the subject of Christian civility.[1] When I set out to write it in the early 1990s, I was inspired by something Lutheran theologian Martin Marty had written in one of his books. People who are civil, he observed, often do not have very strong convictions; and people who have strong convictions often aren't very civil. What we need to cultivate, said Marty, is *convicted civility*.[2]

I was convinced that Marty was right on both counts. On the unconvicted side of things, easygoing relativism seems to abound. Many folks are guided by a "live and let live" mentality, as expressed in a comment like this: "I have my beliefs, and they are true for me. But I don't insist that they have to be true for other people. We all have our own beliefs!"

I find this kind of attitude both confused and dangerous, but in writing a book on the subject of civility, I was more concerned about the other folks that Professor Marty described, the uncivil convicted people—and that is still my main focus. One of the more familiar passages in the Federalist Papers—an important document in American political history—laments the social divisiveness caused by "zeal for different opinions concerning religion."[3] There seems to be a lot of evidence for that concern, not only in North America, but also in other parts of the world. When I set out to write my civility book, Protestants and Catholics were killing each other in Northern Ireland, as were Christians and Muslims in Eastern Europe. We still see the ongoing tensions between Arabs and Jews in the Middle East, as well as serious infighting among different groups within Islam. Additionally, not only have we experienced "culture wars" between Christians and secularists in North America, but we are even seeing much turmoil within Christian denominations.

I designed my book, then, to counteract the incivility of people who, like myself, operate with strong religious convictions. Not long after my book appeared, however, I started getting requests to address other aspects of the incivility syndrome. In one particular ten-day period, for example, reporters from two different major daily newspapers, who were writing stories about civility in American life, interviewed me. It became immediately obvious to me that neither of them actually had read my book; they had simply gotten the word that I was posing as an expert of sorts on the subject. These reporters were not interested in my "big" issues. They wanted to talk about incivility in the ordinary places: road rage on California freeways, angry confrontations between people who want the same parking space, and rude behavior in the aisles of supermarkets.

These reporters were concerned—rightly so—with the most rudimentary patterns of civility, and I was prepared to talk about those rudiments. In my book, I observe that the word "civility" comes from the Greek word for "city" (*civitas*). The public square of the city-state was, for the ancient Greeks, the place where you encountered people who were different from your family and neighbors. This is where strangers gathered, where travelers from other places came to conduct their business. Here one could not rely on the bonds of kinship and friendship. To get along with others, you had to overcome misunderstandings based on different languages and customs. So to be civil was to be "citified"—to know how to treat people decently in the public spaces. It has to do with cultivating good public manners.

Why Good Manners?

I need to say something, though, about the *point* of working at civility. If those of us with strong convictions think cultivating good public manners will make us more likeable, we are in for disillusionment. It is essential to be clear about that at the outset.

If we refuse to back down about what we deeply care about, then simply being nicer is not going to make a lot of folks like us better. Some people will strongly dislike us no matter how good our manners are. I have learned this from experience, so I must speak in personal terms.

I am no card-carrying member of the Religious Right, but I do agree with that movement on important issues. I oppose abortion on demand. I worry about the widespread—and increasingly public—sexual promiscuity in our society. I am troubled about some of the things being taught in public schools. I firmly believe that the word "marriage," even in our increasingly pluralistic society, ought to be restricted to apply to a relationship between a man and a woman.

Since I am known for trying to frame my views in the most civil manner, I am often called upon to defend "conservative" views on moral matters in contexts where those views are not popular. For example, I have spoken on public radio a number of times as an opponent of gay marriage and related matters. I try to make the kindest and gentlest case possible on such occasions. But inevitably, when the time comes for the "call-in listeners," some folks really let me have it. One of the harshest responses to my views was from a person who said that the radio station ought to be ashamed to have someone like me on the air. What's next? he asked. Is the station now going to invite defenders of slavery to air their views?

Many people are deeply offended simply by the fact that people like me have strong views about sexual matters. It does not matter to them whether we put our case as reasonably as possible or whether we simply shout condemnations on the subject. They do not like our views.

It doesn't help to come across as a "balanced" person, even though that is something I work to do. I like the response Rick Warren—the evangelical pastor of "purpose-driven" fame—gave when someone asked him whether he is right wing or left wing. I use both wings, he said, because a one-winged bird can't fly. We need the whole bird. I try to be a whole-bird person. I believe Christians have to care about the poor, about racial justice, about the homeless, about the tendency for governments to move too quickly to military solutions, about how immigrants—both legal and illegal—get treated, and about environmental concerns. I am pleased that many people with theological convictions like mine have begun to pay more attention to some of these issues. We need a bird with two healthy wings!

I also know, though, that I can say all of these "balanced" things over and over again and some folks will still call me a bigot. It comes down to this: I believe strongly in some things with which other people disagree. There is no way of getting around that. Good manners will not automatically improve my image.

It's not that I don't care about image. Good manners may actually get a few of our critics to alter their perceptions of who we are and what we really believe. That would be a plus. But good manners for Christians is something that we must cultivate, even if they do not "work" in getting people to see us—and treat us—differently.

A story made the rounds a few years ago about a meeting that supposedly took place between French and American management leaders. In talking about different approaches to business practices, the French tended to be philosophical and the Americans pragmatic. The difference in their approaches surfaced dramatically in one particular exchange. While one of the Americans outlined a certain management approach, one of the French delegates grew increasingly irritated, and he finally interrupted, "That may work in practice," he exclaimed, "but it will never work in theory!"

That story could be apocryphal, but the point it makes is a good one from a Christian perspective. Not everything that works in practice is compatible with good theory; for Christians, good theory is what fits with biblical teaching.

What I want to offer here is advice about good public manners that I think God wants us to follow. Whether they "work in practice" is a secondary consideration. The real issue is whether we Christians behave in public in a way that pleases our Lord.

Caring about the "Public"

I begin with something basic: *the need to care about public life.* That may strike some as so basic that it hardly needs mentioning, but the fact is that some Christians have considered it a matter of principle *not* to care about what is happening in the public arena. This was true of much of the evangelical community I knew when I was growing up. We were often told that getting involved in "social action" was not the kind of thing God wanted from us. One of the favorite lines I heard from preachers as a kid was that trying to improve things here on earth is like trying to rearrange the deck chairs on the Titanic. The proper attitude that we should have toward "this world" was summed up nicely in a song we often sang:

This world is not my home; I'm just a-passing through.
My treasures are laid up somewhere beyond the blue.
The angels beckon me from heaven's open door,
And I can't feel at home in this world anymore.

Of course, many of the folks who once bought into that view have gotten more involved in public life. Much of this involvement is motivated by a strong sense that we are living in dangerous times and that we Christians have to do whatever we can to stem the tide of evil. Also, much of the motivation for this kind of involvement has to do with a perception that we need to protect our rights as Christians to live out a lifestyle that is obedient to the will of God. Much is happening in our culture that makes it difficult, for example, for parents to see to it that their children are not regularly exposed to bad influences.

I have sympathy for the folks who worry about what is happening in the public arena—in schools, on the Internet, in the entertainment industry, and so on. But being good public Christians isn't only about protecting our personal religious rights and expressions. The Bible gives us some broad assignments. One of my favorites is found in the book of Jeremiah, where the children of Israel have been carried off into captivity in the wicked city of Babylon. This is disorienting for them spiritually. They have grown accustomed to living in Jerusalem, where they had a temple for the true worship of God and where the laws of the land were based on what God had revealed to them. Now they have lost all of that, and they wonder how they can still be faithful servants of the true God.

In Jeremiah 29, the prophet brings them a word from the Lord about how they are to handle this new situation. They are to build houses for their families to live in, and they are to plant crops for their livelihood. God also wants them to "multiply there," marrying and producing children. Then he gives them this assignment for their lives as citizens: "But seek the welfare of the city where I have sent you into exile, and pray to the LORD on its behalf, for in its welfare you will find your welfare" (Jer 29:5-7). The Hebrew word for "welfare" here is *shalom*, which is often translated as "peace" but also includes the ideas of justice and righteousness.

In the New Testament, the Apostle Peter tells the church that like those ancient Israelites in Babylon, we are also "aliens and exiles" in the places where we live. He too gives a broad assignment. "Conduct yourselves honorably among the Gentiles," he says, "so that, though they malign you as evildoers, they may see your honorable deeds, and glorify God when he comes to judge" (1 Pet 2:11-12).

There is no way around this. We have to care about the "welfare" of our fellow human beings. They should see us as folks who act "honorably" in their midst.

We must be sure that we are not motivated to engage in public life merely in response to what we see as threats to our Christian values. Those values should include a desire to promote the well-being of other people, including folks with whom we disagree about basic issues.

Waiting It Out

Here is another piece of advice for Christians who need to cultivate good public manners: *work at developing patience.*

I do quite a bit of reading in the history of democratic thought. While the origins of democratic theory and practice lie in ancient Greece and Rome, much of the significant thought on the subject occurred in the past four centuries or so in Great Britain and the United States. Political thinkers past and present disagree on many of the issues, but there is some consensus on at least two key points. One is that democratic politics requires a willingness to work at compromises. The other is that democracy at its best is practiced by leaders who are willing to engage each other in intelligent and reasoned debate about the fundamental issues at stake in a civil society.

I wish I could see more of this intelligent and reasoned give-and-take in our present-day pubic debates. There has never been a time when it is more important for our national community to take an honest look at itself, to reach across the ideological barriers that we have erected, and to find new ways of living together in some semblance of orderly existence.

The Mennonites have a wonderful phrase to describe our present situation as Christians. We are "living in the time of God's *patience.*" I have to remind myself of this constantly, since I am regularly tempted to ask the Lord why he isn't doing more to keep so many bad things from happening in our world. To accept the fact, though, that God has his own reasons for being patient with this sinful world is to recognize that we must in turn model that same patience in important ways.

Patience is an important quality for our involvement in public life, but it takes effort to cultivate patience. It is understandable that if we get genuinely involved in "seeking the welfare" of the larger society in which we live, we will want to succeed in our efforts to bring about good things. At the same time, however, real success in such matters is presently beyond our reach. Let me explain why.

I believe God is truly in charge of the world. The psalmist makes this clear: "The earth is the LORD's and all that is in it, the world, and those who live in it" (Ps 24:1). The Apostle Paul makes the same point with reference to Christ: "for in him all things in heaven and on earth were created, things visible and invisible, whether thrones or dominions or rulers or powers—all things have been created through him and for him. He himself is before all things, and in him all things hold together" (Col 1:16-17).

So there you have it: God in Christ presently rules over all things and over all people. The problem, however, is that many people in the world today do not acknowledge that fact. They do not recognize the authority of Jesus Christ. Indeed, it isn't just that they refuse to acknowledge his authority; they live in ways that openly oppose the ways God wants human beings to live.

Someday all of this will be straightened out. As a Christian, I firmly believe that there is coming a day when Jesus will return and everyone will know that he is the King of kings and Lord of lords. He will appear on the clouds "and every eye will see him" (Rev 1:7).

Given that reality, then, the key questions about our public roles as Christians today are these: How do we act in the meantime? What is our present responsibility as citizens in societies where people do not acknowledge that there is a God who rules over all things?

I find that many Christians regularly act as if there are only two options in answering these questions. Either we think we have to withdraw from any active concern for public life, or we decide to call on our Christian troops to try to take it over, attempting to enforce "Christian" laws and practices. I don't see either of these options as acceptable. I am convinced that we have to explore a third option: one where we try to accomplish some good things even though we know we are not likely to achieve major victories.

It is not our job to win the battle for righteousness. None of us is the Messiah. The world has already been given one supremely excellent Messiah, and he has guaranteed that ultimately everything will be made right. In the meantime, then, we must take advantage of every opportunity to do whatever we can to promote his cause—knowing all the time that the final victory will happen only when the Lord decides that it is ready to happen.

This calls for patience, and not of a passive sort. We need to be patient in well doing, in seeking the welfare of all.

Promoting Truthfulness

Yet another piece of basic advice is this: *we must be lovers of the truth*. This one is fundamental to everything else associated with good manners. I worry greatly about our behavior on this point. Christians often fudge on the truth even as they aggressively claim to oppose falsehood.

I once heard an evangelical leader speak out against a certain group with whom we evangelicals have significant disagreements. I happened to have studied this group's teachings in considerable detail, so I listened carefully to how he made his case against them. Much of what he said was on target, but at one point he seriously misrepresented what the group believed. Later I approached him privately. I told him that I admired his effort to warn his fellow Christians against the group's false teachings, but on one key point he was attributing to them something they had explicitly denied teaching. There is enough bad stuff to criticize in what the group believed, I said, without accusing them of something that is not really a part of their system.

The leader responded angrily, "You intellectuals have the luxury of making all of these nice distinctions! But I don't have time for all your polite stuff! My job is to warn God's people against false teachers. These folks are false teachers and they don't deserve to be treated fairly!" He had a sneer on his face when he said that last word, "fairly."

This leader had adopted an "anything goes" strategy in opposing a group with which he disagrees. He was going to pull out all the stops in opposing them. When you think about it, though, there is something strange about that approach. We want to oppose false teachers because they do not teach things that are true. But if in our attempts to defeat them we play fast and loose with the truth, attributing to them things that they don't in fact teach—and if we don't care whether we have it exactly right or not—then *we* become false teachers: teachers of untruths!

There is a further irony about this win-at-all-costs mentality when dealing with folks with whom we disagree. In my part of the Christian world, I hear a lot of talk about the importance of the Ten Commandments for public morality. I have no complaints about that. The Ten Commandments are the fundamental outline of how God wants human beings to live. I don't know that we can enforce these commandments in our public life today in a legal sense. Not every sin ought to be made illegal. But when we talk about what makes a society go bad, we do well to focus on the Ten Commandments. Even if we cannot back them up by laws, we can certainly use them in our efforts to witness to others about how the Creator wants people to behave.

Here is the irony, though. One of those commandments tells us that God does not like it when we bear false witness to our neighbors. G. K. Chesterton puts it nicely when he writes, "Idolatry is committed not merely by setting up false gods, but also by setting up false devils." God is not honored when we are unfair to people with whom we disagree.

Self-critique

In thinking about civility and public manners, I keep returning to the importance of *self-examination*. We Christians need to take an honest look at our motives. More importantly, we need to take an honest look at our sins. The need to look at ourselves honestly is a basic requirement of the Christian life.

I met a pastor who told me that the previous Sunday he had used in his sermon what he described as my "Whoops!" interpretation of Psalm 139. Since I did not remember recommending such an interpretation, I asked him what he meant. Having read what I said about that psalm in my civility book, he said he was inspired to describe what the psalmist was experiencing as involving a "Whoops!" moment.

This is what he was getting at: I argue in my book *Uncommon Decency* that there is a noticeable change in mood between what the psalmist says in verses 21 and 22 and what he goes on to say in verses 23 and 24. In those first two verses, the psalmist seems to proclaim boldly that he and God are on the same wavelength, working as allies in a battle against the same foes. "Do I not hate those who hate you, O LORD?" he asks. "And do I not loathe those who rise up against you? I hate them with perfect hatred. I count them my enemies."

Then his tone seems to change drastically. This is where, following my interpretation about the change of mood, the preacher sees him saying, "Whoops!" Suddenly the psalmist seems to realize that he has slipped into an arrogant spiritual state and realizes that he has to turn inward. That is when he pleads with the Lord to deal with the sin he finds in his own soul: "Search me, O God," he prays, "and know my heart; test me and know my thoughts. See if there is any wicked way in me, and lead me in the way everlasting."

I don't know whether my "Whoops!" interpretation has it exactly right, but I do know this: We cannot oppose the evil forces that God opposes without also looking for the ways in which those evil forces operate in our own deep places.

Civility does not come easily. It is something we have to work to achieve. But I am convinced that the hard task is taking an honest look at our own inner being. Once we admit to God and others what we find there, it is easier to approach the sins of others with a sense that we share at least some important things in common.

Civility as "Art Appreciation"

In 1923, the Roman Catholic Church officially elevated Therese of Lisieux to sainthood, but she would have been a special saint in my estimation even if Rome had not made that decision. Her spiritual journal is one of my favorite books.[4]

Therese was an amazing person. Born in 1873, she entered a Carmelite convent at the age of fifteen and died when she was only twenty-four.

During her short life, though, she recorded some profound thoughts about her relationship with Christ, to whom she was deeply committed.

Therese worked hard at empathy, which I see as a key component in civility. Empathy is the capacity to identify with other people by trying to understand them from their "inside"—the word "empathy" literally means "in feeling"—and not simply seeing them in a way shaped by our own biases. Therese considered the cultivating of empathy as a special sort of spiritual obligation, and she regularly called on Jesus for help in her assignment. Here she describes the effort as it applied to an especially disagreeable member of her religious community:

> [O]ne of the nuns managed to irritate me whatever she did or said. The devil was mixed up in it, for it was certainly he who made me see so many disagreeable traits in her. As I did not want to give way to my natural dislike of her, I told myself that charity should not only be a matter of feeling but should show itself in deeds. So I set myself to do for this sister just what I should have done for someone I loved most dearly. Every time I met her, I prayed for her and offered God all her virtues and her merits. I was sure this would greatly delight Jesus, for every artist likes to have his works praised and the divine Artist of souls is pleased when we do not halt outside the exterior of the sanctuary where He has chosen to dwell but go inside and admire its beauty.[5]

I find Saint Therese's image here of Jesus as the divine artist to be especially helpful. For Christians, coming to experience our solidarity with other human beings—especially those with whom we are inclined to differ on important matters—is a process something like an exercise in art appreciation. Art appreciation, in the straightforward sense of the term, comes more easily to some of us than to others. But for most of us, I suspect, it is something we need to work hard at cultivating. I have special reasons for confessing my lack of proper cultivation in this area. My wife is trained as an art historian, and our son says this means his father has sat waiting on the steps of some of the great art museums of the world! I have to work hard at art appreciation.

Civility, the capacity to show good manners, especially toward those with whom we disagree on important matters, requires something like the sensitivities of art appreciation. We know that in the aesthetic realm the reason the requisite sensitivities do not come easily for most of us is due in part to the fact—when it comes to being able to appreciate a Picasso or a Warhol or a Nevelson—that we have not studied the subject enough.

The need to study what we are being asked to appreciate is also necessary in the case of human relationships, but here the factor of human sinfulness is also obviously a matter that we have to address. We live under the curse of Babel: we erect barriers that separate us from others, and our sinfulness reinforces our desire to work hard at making sure those barriers are not broken down. For Christians the situation is compounded by the fact that the barriers are often necessitated by significant disagreements. Slipping into anything-goes relativism is no solution. Many of the barriers that separate us should loom large in our Christian consciousness. They actually mark off boundaries of behavior and belief that signal deep and important differences having to do with our competing understandings of the human condition.

But no Christian can simply leave it there. The biblical mandate is clear: "if it is possible, so far as it depends on you, live peaceably with all" (Rom 12:18). "Always be ready to make your defense to anyone who demands from you an account of the hope that is in you," the Apostle Peter tells us; but he immediately adds, "yet do it with gentleness and reverence" (1 Pet 3:15-16).

Again, this is no easy task. Therese of Lisieux was right to call on the Lord for help in cultivating empathy. Sometimes what it comes down to is recognition that God sees the person we consider so difficult with a love that we cannot fathom. All we can do, then, is to treat the person as someone who is loved by God.

I once heard a priest tell a story about Pope John XIII when he was still an Italian cardinal. He was having dinner one night with a priestly assistant who was reporting to him about another priest, a real renegade who was doing things that were embarrassing the hierarchy. The future pope listened calmly, sipping wine from a goblet. Finally the assistant cried out in a frustrated tone, "How can you take this so calmly? Don't you realize what this priest is doing?" The cardinal then gently asked the younger priest, "Father, whose goblet is this?" "It is yours, your grace," the priest answered. The cardinal then threw the goblet to the floor, and it shattered into many fragments. "And now whose goblet is it?" he asked. "It is still yours," was the answer. "And so is this priest still my brother in Christ," said the cardinal, "even though he is shattered and broken."

God created all human beings. Even the shattered and broken ones are his original works of art.

No Limits?

This is a point, of course, where serious questions start to nag some folks about the need for civility. How far do we go in cultivating empathy toward folks with whom we disagree? Are there no limits to the obligation to be civil?

My answer is that there are indeed limits. Take the obvious kinds of cases, some of the real villains in human history. Do I want to insist that the broken goblet story should be applied to a Hitler or a Saddam Hussein? As a recommendation about how to treat them, definitely not. They are wicked men who have caused unspeakable harm. They do not deserve civility. People like them need to be opposed, and in opposing them we ought not to waste any time cultivating empathy for them.

Those are, of course, the extreme cases—situations in which certain individuals are so given over to evil that no degree of civility is going to curtail their wicked designs. But there are even less extreme cases where a limit has been reached in our efforts to be civil. I often find myself reaching those limits. Sometimes I simply have to take sides against someone whose wrong actions or ideas affect the lives and hearts of many people. A line has been drawn in the sand, and no impulse toward civility will allow me to cross it in good conscience. I hope I am as clear as I can be about this: the quest for civility has limits; there are times in life when civility is no longer possible.

Having said that as clearly as I can, I need to add a "however" clause. None of this should serve as an excuse for not making sure that we have genuinely explored the possibilities of civility in many specific cases. There may come a time to set aside good manners, but that does not mean we should set them aside too quickly.

My theology tells me that no human being is beyond redemption until that human being has taken a final breath. Recently I was forced to wrestle with my theology on that subject in a special way. We spent the 2007–2008 academic year at Fuller Seminary celebrating our founding in 1947. During that anniversary year, we adopted the old gospel hymn, "To God Be the Glory, Great Things He Has Done," as the one we would sing at our special anniversary events. I had many occasions, then, to think about the theology of the last two lines of Fanny Crosby's third verse of that hymn: "The vilest offender who truly believes, / That moment from Jesus a pardon receives."

The theological message there is clear. Those "vilest offenders" whom I singled out—folks like Hitler and Saddam Hussein—are not beyond the scope of redemption if they come to a point in their lives where they "truly believe." At that point, they receive a full pardon for their sins because of what Jesus did on the cross.

I struggle with that thought, but ultimately I have to yield to it. Indeed, it helps to remind myself that I too am a vile offender, completely undeserving of the salvation I have been offered by God's grace. This means I cannot completely give up on anyone else who is still alive. If they repent of their sins, God will graciously redeem them.

That does not mean, of course, that I have to compromise my Christian witness by accepting any opportunity to show civility toward vile offenders. Suppose, for example, that radio "shock jock" Howard Stern, well known for his blasphemous and pornographic shenanigans, were to invite me onto his program for an interview. I would turn him down. I would not want to give the impression that I in any way endorse or encourage his wickedness. But if I had the opportunity to meet with him privately, I would show him Christian civility in the hope that we might be able to speak together about matters that are important for the eternal well-being of each of our souls.

Offering Hospitality

I was talking with an old friend, a gifted theologian, and I asked him what he was working on these days. The theology of hospitality, he answered. Then he made this fascinating observation. God's creating the world, he said, was the first act of hospitality. Being hospitable, he explained, is making space for people or things, even when you are not obliged to do so. God was not obliged to create the world. God, as God, is totally self-sufficient. He does not need us. Yet God chose to create, to make room for the likes of us. We have a hospitable God.

Not long after that conversation, I read a marvelous book on Christian hospitality by Christine Pohl, who teaches ethics at Asbury Theological Seminary. The title she chose for her book—*Making Room*—reinforced the point my theologian friend had made. In the most direct sense, hospitality is taking the *needs* of others seriously. We are being hospitable when we give weary ones a place to sleep and when we make room at our tables for people to share our food.

As Christine Pohl points out, though, the word "hospitality" has been robbed of its original core meaning in recent times. We talk much about the "hospitality industry," referring thereby to "hotels and restaurants which are open to strangers as long as they have money or credit cards."[6] True hospitality goes much deeper than an economic transaction. It is graciously making room in our lives for other people and their needs.

We can think of civility as a form of hospitality. It is making room for other people, for their hopes and fears; it is a willingness to create a space in our minds for their ideas and experiences, for showing empathy for what is going on in their lives, even when strictly speaking we are not obligated to do so.

Jesus showed a literal hospitality to people whose lifestyles and ideas he strongly opposed. This is what got him into trouble with the religious leaders of his day: "The Pharisees and their scribes were complaining to his disciples, saying, 'Why do you eat and drink with tax collectors and sinners?'" (Luke 5:30). I can understand something of the concerns of those religious leaders. A genuine vulnerability often comes with a hospitable spirit. The same holds for a willingness to "make room" for the ideas and experiences of those with whom we disagree on serious matters. But we need to take the risks.

Once I gave a talk to a good-sized audience on a large university campus. I spoke on the subject of civility. The folks who sponsored my lecture were from several campus ministry groups, many of them evangelical. There had been some controversy over "culture wars" issues on that campus in recent months, and they asked me to address questions about how we can best deal with public controversies in a Christian spirit. One point I made with a special emphasis was the need to talk with our opponents face to face, whenever possible, before going public with our criticisms.

Afterward, the leaders of one of the evangelical campus groups came up to talk with me. They told me how they had run ads in the campus newspaper stating the evangelical understanding of sexual fidelity, with some mention of their opposition to same-sex relationships. One of the gay-lesbian groups had countered with an angry published response, and they had gone back and forth a bit, trading letters to the editor. "It has gotten a bit out of hand," the leaders said. "Realistically, from your point of view, how should we have handled it differently?"

I told them that I thought they should have asked for a private meeting with the gay-lesbian leaders at the outset. They should have shown them the ads and said, "We know you will disagree with our position, but we do want you to see this ahead of time. And if there is anything in here that you think seriously misrepresents your point of view, we want to know about it. We want to say what we believe, but we do not want to be needlessly offensive in doing so."

The evangelical leaders thanked me for my advice, and they told me they wished they had done the kind of thing I proposed.

Several weeks later, I received a note from one of them. "After we talked with you," they said, "we met with the leaders of the gay-lesbian group—we invited them to lunch, and they accepted," he reported. "We told them that we wish that we had contacted them privately before running our ad. We apologized for how we have typically gone about making our views known, and we asked their forgiveness. It started off awkward, but by the end of the conversation we were talking about other stuff, and then they said we should meet again, and the next time lunch was on them. I think we are on a new path—not compromising, but making our case in a kinder way!"

This group was taking some important risks in cultivating civility. I was proud of them for what they had done. They were learning good manners!

The Spiritual Dimension

I was indeed proud of those campus ministry folks for reaching out in the way they did to those with whom they disagreed about sexuality. They did a good thing, and it wasn't easy for them.

What made their reaching out especially difficult, though, was the fact that they did so *after* the public controversy had occurred. It would have been easier to arrange that lunch if they had done it *before* they published their ads. This leads me to wonder why they did not think to take that step. When they came to me for advice, they seemed genuinely stymied about what they might have done to lessen the tensions while still being forthright in expressing their convictions. When I proposed to them that they might have arranged a private conversation before going public, it was clearly an "Aha!" experience for them. I suggested something they had not considered.

This leads me to wonder why. Why are we Christians so often reluctant to reach out to others with whom we disagree? Why do we seem to many non-Christians like arrogant and intolerant people?

The answer I keep coming back to is that it is a failure of spirituality. We have not seen public manners, the cultivating of civility, as an important element in our spiritual formation. In a way, that does not surprise me. Spirituality in general—which includes taking on the disciplines of prayer, reflection, the devotional study of the Scriptures in order to immerse ourselves in the stories of those of the past who have found the sources of spiritual strength—is difficult stuff. It doesn't come easily. I know that personally. When it comes to spiritual laziness, I am a chief of sinners.

To say that the cultivation of civility is a spiritual matter, then, does not suddenly solve the problem. It merely points to the larger spiritual agenda on which we all need to work. We must add civility to an agenda that is already full of difficult challenges. It is a step forward, however, simply to acknowledge that cultivating civility, learning good public manners, is indeed on that agenda.

Notes

1. Richard J. Mouw, *Uncommon Decency: Christian Civility in an Uncivil World* (Downers Grove IL: InterVarsity Press, 1992).

2. Martin E. Marty, *By Way of Response* (Nashville: Abingdon Press, 1981) 81.

3. The Federalist Papers, selected and edited by Roy P. Fairfield (Garden City NY: Anchor Books, 1961) 18–19.

4. *The Autobiography of Saint Therese of Lisieux: The Story of a Soul,* trans. John Beevers (New York: Doubleday, 1957).

5. Ibid., 126–27.

6. Christine D. Pohl, *Making Room: Recovering Hospitality as a Christian Tradition* (Grand Rapids MI: Wm. B. Eerdmans Publishing Co., 1999) 4.

Chapter 3

What We Need Is More Maturity

Stacy F. Sauls,
Bishop of Episcopal Diocese of Lexington, Kentucky

The Church in Anxious Times

This reflection on civility and the church has a context. It is unavoidably written from the perspective of a bishop of the Episcopal Church dealing on a daily basis with the challenges it faces, two of which are the issues of human sexuality and the concerns for church unity for which sexuality issues are the occasion. Both are perceived as highly threatening to our identity as a church.[1] Anxiety is the instinctive response to threat, and the challenges we face have resulted in no small amount of anxiety, both for the Episcopal Church and the Anglican Communion of which it is a part.

To complicate matters further, issues of human sexuality, and homosexuality in particular, go beyond rational questions of biblical interpretation, church tradition, and Christian ethics, and get at something far more instinctual. In addition to being the subject of deep cultural taboos, sexuality is a basic issue of survival; a function rooted more in the brain stem than the cerebral cortex. The anxiety surrounding sex is challenging under the best of circumstances, but the disagreements among the member churches of the Anglican Communion and the virulence of those disagreements, the fundamental importance of unity as a matter of faith,[2] and the important reality that what is at stake are real human relationships all intensify the anxiety.

If changes in understanding related to sexuality were the first changes the Episcopal Church had dealt with in a long time, that would be one thing. They are not. Sexuality comes on the heels of the most extensive revisions to the church's Book of Common Prayer[3] since its inception, and the ordination of women with its profound implications for the reordering of the church and, indeed, humanity itself. Change is by definition threatening to the way things are and, in this case, seemingly always have been. Threat yields anxiety.

Change in the Episcopal Church is, of course, only part of the phenomenon of change in the church universal. As we move into a postmodern reality, we can only guess at the full extent of that change. We can, however, see some of its effects.

All of the mainline denominations in the United States are experiencing decline in membership.[4] Even our country's largest Protestant denomination, Southern Baptists, is beginning to experience such decline.[5] Furthermore, the privileged place of religion in American life, especially of Christianity, can no longer be assumed. In fact, American culture in this postmodern world shows signs of a decided hostility to religion in general and Christianity in particular. There are signs of a distancing from religion at the highest levels. Both of the 2008 presidential candidates, John McCain and Barack Obama, distanced themselves from religious leaders, the former by rejecting endorsements from certain evangelical pastors and the latter by resigning membership in his church. The Supreme Court has shown signs of weakening the status of religion in American life under both the Free Exercise Clause[6] and the Establishment Clause of the First Amendment.[7]

Change in the life of the church is not happening in isolation. The culture as a whole is changing. Change itself is changing in that it is more rapid than at any time in human history.[8] It is no wonder that the environment in which we live is marked by a pervasive sense of apprehension and unease. Anxiety feeds anxiety.

Anxiety, of course, though uncomfortable, is not necessarily a bad thing. It serves a useful function by motivating us to respond to danger. The problem is that it is instinctive, and instinct may not lead us to the most appropriate response to a given threat, particularly more complex threats. The instinctively anxious response by gorillas to gather together when threatened by a leopard is entirely appropriate to survival, but their gathering is distinctly inappropriate to survival in response to a threat from a human hunter with a rifle. Human beings have the capacity to respond to perceived threats more intelligently than instinct might at first suggest, but we do not do so effortlessly. The capacity for higher-level thinking does us no good if anxious instinct inhibits us from getting to it. What matters is the ability to get beyond instinct to the higher-level thinking, and indeed to resist instinct in order to get there. That is a matter of maturity.

Anxiety and the maturity of response to it, I believe, have much to do with the topic of this collection of essays, civility in the church. I have witnessed civility, both in the sense of a breakdown in manners and in the higher sense of concern for the common good, sorely tested by our anxious reactivity, which leads to the most instinctive animal reactions to threat— fight or flight—both of which can be observed in church life. I have witnessed those I know to have impeccable manners fight in the name of God with opponents in the most atrocious ways, more appropriate for the gutter than the sanctuary.[9] I have witnessed others, also in the name of God, break all relationship with those with whom they disagree, usually blaming those left behind as they leave and often continuing to fight even after they've left.

My Southern mother would have said, "Their mamas would be ashamed," but the antidote to incivility, I'm afraid, is more complex than an infusion of manners. What we need here, I'm convinced, is not more manners. It is more maturity, and that is a great deal more elusive.

By maturity I mean the ability to take responsibility for one's emotional being and destiny. One aspect of responsibility for one's emotional being is the ability to rise above the instinctual emotional response to anxiety and employ higher-level thinking in response to what is threatening. A corollary is the ability to allow others to take responsibility for their emotional being and destiny; in other words, to know one's boundaries, where one ends and another begins, and to respect those boundaries. The problem we face as a church, more than anything else, is fostering the maturity we need, especially when a highly anxious environment works against it.

The Presence of Maturity and Immaturity Among Us

The Episcopal Church's current context is unavoidably the place where my personal reflection begins and out of which I hope to suggest some positive ways forward. Our recent history provides an excellent illustration of the difference between a mature response to the challenges and an immature one.

On August 5, 2003, the General Convention of the Episcopal Church met in Minneapolis. It was the day the bishops of our church were to consider the approval of a partnered gay man who was duly elected to be a bishop following a delay due to an unfounded last-minute allegation of his misconduct. The laity and other clergy had approved his election two days earlier. It was a highly anxious environment.

After a prayerful period of discernment based on the principles of Ignatian spirituality, we discussed the issue among ourselves. Some were in favor; some opposed. We concluded our deliberations with prayers for healing and reconciliation, which included an anointing with oil and a laying on of hands. As we approached the stations at which this sacramental sign of our wholeness in Christ was taking place, I noticed something important. Two bishops of our church, one female and one male, each of whom had been on the task force charged with studying the issue and presenting their results to us earlier in the year and each of whom was considered to be an outspoken advocate of opposite positions, approached one of the stations together, side by side and holding hands. It was, I thought at the time, the essence of maturity. Each took responsibility for himself or herself, each respected the integrity of the other, and each avoided taking responsibility for the other, including the theological opinion of the other. In the moment of uncertainty about what our deliberations would yield, it filled me with hope for our future.

After the bishops had reached a decision concurring with that of the clergy and laity and thus clearing the way for the first openly partnered gay bishop, another of my colleagues asked to address us. Though we were about to adjourn for the day, permission was granted. That bishop took the microphone at the podium, which is contrary to the normal custom of addressing our peers from the table at which we are seated. "Today," he said, "the House has abandoned the clear teaching of Scripture." The moment he uttered the words, my heart sank. It was the opposite of what I had witnessed earlier. The bishop addressing us, the self-designated leader of the opposition to our action, admitted no possibility that anyone could legitimately and faithfully disagree with him. Immaturity cannot accept the reasonableness of disagreement. Maturity can.

Where does that leave us? If we abandon the *clear* teaching of Scripture, that means we must either be so stupid that we cannot understand what is clear, so evil that we do not care what is clear, or both. It is not surprising that incivility on every level followed, both personal incivility in that we treated each other shamefully, and incivility in the higher sense in that we tore the community apart.

The Immaturity of Clearness Thinking

If you think about it, clearness thinking is almost always erroneous. If things were really clear, people would not argue about them so earnestly. What we hear is a lot of talk such as "the Bible *clearly* says" or "the truth is *clear*," or "anyone who disagrees is *clearly* homophobic," or "anyone who disagrees is *clearly* heretical," or "justice *clearly* requires." Clearness thinking is a way of insisting on agreement where agreement does not otherwise exist. The missing quality is not intelligence because people of equal intelligence engage in it. It is not good will because people of equal good will engage in it. It is not faithfulness or commitment, because equally devoted people engage in it. It is not associated with one side of the issues or the other because people of all opinions on the issues engage in it. It is not manners because people of impeccable manners engage in it. The missing quality is maturity.

Disagreements about the truth, when the truth is not clear, are not new to us. It was so regarding the necessity of circumcision in the first century (Acts 15). It was so regarding the divine rights of kings in 1533 (Henry VIII), 1649 (Charles I), and 1776 (George III). It was so regarding slavery in 1860. We should not be surprised that, at least at the moment, we cannot be of one mind. This may, of course, be painful in the short run. In the long run, though, the issues that have caused us pain in the past have found their resolution eventually. Maturity is necessary in order to seek the truth when truth is not clear and when the instinctual reaction is to relieve the pain caused by lack of clarity.

The fact that truth is not clear, of course, does not mean truth does not exist. It only means we must work harder to find it. It may mean it will take longer to find it. It may well be that none of us is right, at least entirely. It is possible, though, to disagree and still be civil. It is possible that disagreement should actually encourage civility because it highlights our need for each other to solve a difficult problem for the common good, which is civility in its highest sense.

The essence of the problem with clearness thinking is that it is immature. Immaturity resorts to one of two approaches. It must resolve the discomfort of disagreement either by forcing agreement or by separating. Both are simplistic solutions to complex challenges, and neither exhibits the maturity we so badly need. Attempts to resolve the conflict either by enforcing uniformity or separating are both premature and immature, and they are not characteristically Anglican. Our history suggests a more mature alternative.

Seeing the Maturity in Conflicts of the Past

The good news of church conflict is that it suggests that there are Christian men and women motivated by faith and by love—love of God, love of the church, and love of people, including gay people—who care enough to seek the truth, even when it involves struggle and pain. I do not think we could ask for more than that. The task before us is to encourage them and not to try to stop them. It will not be quick. It will not be easy. It will not be clear. It will be mature, and it will be in the interests of civility in every sense.

What we need now is to make the most possible room for maturity to emerge among us. Instead of trying to draw us closer together or to separate us, as clearness thinking unavoidably does, I am convinced that the wiser and more mature approach would be to give us more space, more room to be different, at least for now. Our history as a church has some salutary examples of precisely this approach.

One involves a matter of eucharistic theology. It would be difficult to imagine a more basic issue to the church's self-understanding. Even with this issue, indeed *especially* with this issue, the origins of Anglicanism found a way not only to tolerate diversity, and by implication error, but to encourage it in the interests of the well-being of the whole, *i.e.,* to show civility.

The understanding of the Holy Eucharist, like the violence of the English Reformation itself, swung on a pendulum between Catholicism and Protestantism. Those were the good old days of civility in the church when people literally were killing themselves all over Europe over whether a little piece of bread actually became the body of Christ or was merely a reminder of the Last Supper.

The first Prayer Book of King Edward VI in 1549 exhibited a Catholic understanding of the Eucharist in the words the priest was instructed to say during the administration of the bread: "The body of our Lord Jesus Christ, which was given for thee, preserve thy body and soul unto everlasting life." By the second Prayer Book of Edward the VI in 1552, the English Reformation had taken a more Protestant turn. The former words of administration were replaced by a new formula: "Take and eat this in remembrance that Christ died for thee, and feed on him in thy heart by faith, with thanksgiving." Those words were rewritten after Edward's death under his successor and sister, the devout Roman Catholic Queen Mary, in whose reign Edward's archbishop of Canterbury and author of the Prayer Book, Thomas Cranmer, was not only replaced but martyred. When it comes to theology, killing one another over what the Eucharist means has a certain undeniable logical consistency, whatever it may lack in civility.

Queen Elizabeth I, who in turn succeeded Mary, recognized that the clearness thinking of the Reformation, and its necessary implication that some people were stupid, evil, or both, threatened to undermine English civilization. Her insight, indeed genius in my opinion, was to recognize that civility was not well served by premature orthodoxy and that faithfulness might make room for more than one way, at least for some time. Thus, Elizabeth's Prayer Book of 1559 opted neither for the Catholic formula of the 1549 book or the Protestant formula of the 1552 book. Instead, it put the two formulae together in a beautiful and poetic, if long, statement that allowed completely inconsistent understandings of what the Eucharist means to exist at the same time: "The Body of our Lord Jesus Christ, which was given for thee, preserve thy body and soul unto everlasting life. Take and eat this in remembrance that Christ died for thee, and feed on him in thy heart by faith, with thanksgiving." These words remain a part of the Episcopal Church's Book of Common Prayer, as well as that of the Church of England, to this day. They are inherently civil words. They are civil words because they encourage respect for human beings across theological divides. They are civil words because they encourage relationship beyond rational consistency. They are civil words because they encourage peace in the church instead of counterproductive conflict. They are civil because they facilitate the emerging of truth in God's time rather than yielding to human impatience. They are mature words because they recognize that allowing another to believe according to conscience preserves rather than threatens one's own right to believe according to conscience.

I am not suggesting that the Eucharist can actually mean two logically inconsistent things, and I don't think Elizabeth was suggesting that either. I am suggesting that the best way to seek the truth of the Eucharist in a situation when the truth is manifestly not clear, as evidenced by how many people disagree about it, might be to allow inconsistent understandings to coexist, even if it takes a long time. In fact, over the history of Anglicanism, a common understanding has in fact emerged so that our official position is now the same as that of Roman Catholicism.[10] The difference from Roman Catholicism is the way in which our communal understanding of the truth came to be. However Catholics may have arrived at theirs, Anglicans could not have arrived at their now settled understanding without considerable forbearance and maturity.

There is another instructive and highly relevant, as well as more recent, example in our past. Almost throughout its history, the Episcopal Church has struggled with the issue of allowing remarriage after divorce. We began at the General Convention of 1808 and did not finally resolve the issue until 1973. It is an issue that, like the current issues of sexuality with which we are dealing, involves sexual ethics, biblical interpretation (arguably much clearer than interpretations regarding homosexuality), and the nature of Christian marriage.

Though it is difficult for us from a perspective 200 years later to imagine the controversy that surrounded this issue, the reality is that the matter was highly contentious and occupied huge amounts of the General Convention's time at virtually every meeting after 1808 until 1946. Until that point, the General Convention had attempted to define a position in advance of a consensus emerging. What happened in 1946 is that the convention, perhaps inadvertently, passed a canon that allowed inconsistency to prevail provisionally, which had the effect of maturely respecting differences of opinion while the issue naturally resolved itself in the hearts and minds of the people.

The 1946 canon provided that any member of the Church whose marriage had been annulled or dissolved or who desired to marry a person whose marriage had been annulled or dissolved might apply to the bishop "for a judgment as to his or her marital status in the eyes of the Church." The judgment could in turn be granted "when any of the facts set forth [*i.e.,* impediments to marriage justifying an annulment] are shown *to exist or to have existed* which manifestly establish that no marriage bond as the same is recognized by this Church exists."[11] The ambiguity of the words "to exist or to have existed" resulted in an interesting situation. It allowed some bishops to approve remarriage only when an impediment to marriage was found "to have existed" before the marriage was entered. It also allowed other bishops to approve remarriage when an impediment to marriage was found "to exist" at the time the permission was sought, whether or not it existed before the marriage was entered. Attempts were made, but rejected, to resolve the inconsistency. Instead, the church lived with the inconsistency, which was not unlike that of the 1559 Prayer Book, for almost thirty years while the issue resolved itself. In 1973, the Episcopal Church enacted a canon allowing for remarriage after divorce with the permission of a bishop virtually without dissent and without a disruption to unity. It is an understanding, by the way, that almost all Anglican churches in the world have come to, even the most outspoken in their opposition to same-sex relationships.[12] Given room, Anglicans have a tendency to find a common understanding with maturity.

Tolerance for Conflict Encourages Maturity to Emerge

One of the great challenges before us, and one that I fear not everyone at the highest levels of leadership in our church understands, is not to resolve conflict prematurely. Our communion is relatively young, but our history suggests that premature resolution will not serve us well. In the life of the church, even 450 years is not a long time, but the truth is that while the Church of England may have had an existence independent of Rome for that long, this fellowship of independent churches known as the Anglican Communion is much younger, 220 years if you reckon its beginning from the birth of the first church related to the Church of England but not subject to it (the Episcopal Church, which came into being after the American Revolution), and a mere 140 years if you reckon its beginning from the calling of the first Lambeth Conference. Even more recent dates for its beginning are plausible.

From that perspective, what our history suggests is that the disagreement among us, even its virulence, may not be so different from that between siblings as they grow up in a family. Being an only child, I found as a father that my sons' fighting among themselves made me deeply uncomfortable, a discomfort I was inclined to resolve by sending both of them to their respective rooms to restore the peace. As I became more tolerant of my own discomfort and matured as a father, I came to realize that my sons' growing up depended on allowing them the room they needed to fight it out (as long as I kept them from killing each other). Our historical experience, particularly regarding eucharistic theology and remarriage after divorce, suggests that what is needed right now is the maturity to allow enough room to fight it out while contained in an environment that will not allow us to kill each other. Neither discomfort nor pain is such a bad thing. After all, they are how human beings get motivated to grow up.

At least part of the difficulty with finding the room we need to work out our sibling differences is the increasing reality of the multicultural nature of Anglicanism. The majority of Anglicans, which is the third largest of Christian traditions, are neither English nor white. They are African and black, and that reality is understandably asserting itself. It is also understandably asserting itself in opposition to the colonial experience that sought to subjugate it, and perhaps still does. That reality is further complicated by the fact that, due to the nature of electronic communications, the multiple cultures in which Anglicans live out their faith today frequently are squeezed together in conflict rather than given room to be themselves. What happens on one side of the world is known instantly on the other as if those two contexts were not as different as they are. The potential for misunderstanding is huge and indeed is subject to exploitation by those with divisive motives. That the world is shrinking carries with it the definite advantage of distant cultures enriching our own, and vice versa. That the world in shrinking carries with it the definite disadvantage of making assumptions of meaning that distort thought and lead to serious misunderstandings. Instantaneous communication has a tendency to promote the instinctual and reactive to the detriment of the mature and reflective.

Our history may suggest a solution to that as well: how even in a world of instant communications, we can give ourselves the space we need to work through our problems without either forcing conformity or requiring separation. The second pillar of Elizabeth's resolution of the English Reformation, which went hand in hand with the toleration evidenced in the issue of eucharistic theology, is the principle of local autonomy.[13] One of the great dangers facing us at the moment is the temptation to discard the wisdom of local autonomy, which gives us room to work out our issues in the face of cross-cultural differences instead of resorting to quick-fix solutions that seek to avoid our conflicts by drawing us closer together without due regard for those differences.

It is a basic precept of Anglicanism that the local church should be governed locally. Anglicanism knows no universal jurisdiction like that of the Bishop of Rome in Catholicism, which is another approach to the same problem. That means the monarch is the supreme governor of the Church of England. The General Convention is the supreme governor of the Episcopal Church. The other provinces of the Anglican Communion are similarly governed autonomously in accordance with local context and custom. Until recently, that principle has been universally respected.

Elizabeth paved the way for a mature way of dealing with multiculturalism. Whereas Catholicism promotes uniformity emanating from Rome, Anglicanism promotes diversity based on local culture, tradition, and context. The fellowship is universal in Holy Baptism, but the governance is local in autonomy. It allows, when it works, a community that is more like a fruit salad than a fruit smoothie, a community in which the individual parts are related but respected in their individuality rather than homogenized into a perhaps more easily digested sameness. African expressions of faith will differ from Asian expressions of faith, which will differ from European expressions of faith, which will differ from American expressions of faith, which will differ from Pacific Islander expressions of faith, which will differ from Aboriginal expressions of faith. Elizabeth's genius is what allows the diversity to stay in relationship without being suppressed. Autonomy promotes maturity because it respects boundaries, where one ends and another begins. It is admittedly messier than the Roman approach of a magisterium or the approach of confessional Protestantism, which sacrifices individuality for a common doctrinal statement. Maturity not only encourages, but thrives, on individuality.

Three Practical Suggestions to Encourage the Emergence of Maturity

The challenge is that we live in a time when being mature is getting harder and harder to do. We are living through a period in history, perhaps not all that unlike others, when religious controversy, precisely because of how important religion is to us at a deep level, may not encourage the maturity we so badly need.

I have three suggestions to make. The first is to frame our situation in terms of a spiritual discipline that inherently encourages maturity—the Benedictine practice of hospitality.

My observation is that all the rational thinking in the world is not going to resolve the issues regarding homosexuality, at least not right now. A lot of apparently rational thinking has gone into resolving them up to this point. More ink has been spilled than we can quantify in attempting to do so. The word *clear* has appeared more times than can be counted, and we are no closer to a resolution than we ever have been.

The rational will work itself out in time, but it cannot do so, or at least is much less likely to do so, unless we focus on the relational first. In order for truth to emerge, it is a prior necessity that we step away for the moment from trying to determine what the truth is, or even worse, who has it, and concentrate instead on making room for those who see the truth differently than we do. I am not saying that any of us should abandon the search for truth. I am saying that it would serve the interests of truth to concentrate first on love, on how we can live together, on how we make room for one another. That is an issue of hospitality.

Hospitality is a spiritual practice founded in no less than the love of Christ. There can be nothing more closely related to the Christian faith than love. It is in welcoming each other as if we were strangers, and our differences have nearly made us so, that the practice of hospitality might well lead us to encounter Christ, the beloved, in each other. To encounter Christ in each other is to be open and connected in a new way. At a time of deep division over the truth, hospitality offers us as Christians a way to welcome the stranger, even the ideological or the theological stranger, which we have surely become to each other. Welcoming the stranger offers the opportunity for an encounter with love in both the biblical[14] and Benedictine traditions.[15] Love converts our hearts, and conversion opens our minds to the emergence of truth. Hospitality may allow our transformation in the gospel to occur. But Christian hospitality, at its deepest, receives the other as other. It does not confuse self with other, and that brings us back to maturity.

The reality that all human beings are made in God's image (Gen 1:27) and our love for God are the foundations of the practice of hospitality that may make the room for each other that we so badly need. Not only those of us who have the truth are God's image. There is no scriptural qualification to the *imago dei*. It is borne by all of us, friend and stranger alike, and theological stranger as well. Honor and reverence must be the hallmark of our relations. We must meet each other with compassion and a willingness to bear one another's burdens, maybe even one another's errors. Neither being right nor possessing the truth is a qualification on our mutual compassion any more than it is a qualification on the *imago dei*. "Bearing God's image establishes for every person a fundamental dignity which cannot be undermined by wrongdoing . . . or neediness . . . . Humanness itself requires that persons recognize others as like themselves."[16]

Perhaps it is in our common error that we can most recognize our common humanity, and perhaps it is in recognizing our common humanity that we can most recognize God. Perhaps it is indeed the stranger of the greatest error on the issue of homosexuality who presents to us the greatest potential for encountering God precisely because this stranger offers the greatest spiritual opportunity for the showing of hospitality. Indeed, the greater the error and the greater the ideological divide, the greater the opportunity for Christ, who is both same and other, to be present to us. Our differences from one another, our disagreements, and our strangeness should not drive us apart. They should draw us together most strongly in hospitality. They should offer the greatest spiritual opportunity for us and not the greatest spiritual threat. It is paradoxical thinking, to be sure. Paradox, though, is often where God seems to reside.

The second suggestion is missional. Doctrinal controversy is something we take seriously, often with deadly seriousness. Deadly seriousness may not be the best place from which to encourage maturity, since it is not always conducive to our best thinking and tends to push us toward the instinctive, which is our most serious place of all, the place where our survival needs reside.

Mission might be the adventurous antidote to anxious seriousness and a way to overcome our doctrinal differences, even if only provisionally, for the good of God's people. Mission might allow us to encounter freely and serendipitously what God has in store for us.

Doctrinal controversy has been juxtaposed with mission for me recently. In summer 2008 I made two overseas trips. The first one was to South Africa where my diocese has a partnership with a South African diocese and an order of Anglican Benedictine monks for the sake of mission. The project is a reading camp like the ones we've been doing in my diocese now for seven years. We brought eighteen eight-to-ten-year-olds together for a week of fun camp activities and intensive remedial work in reading skills done in a way that resembles a traditional school setting as little as possible and integrates reading as part of summer camp life. The whole idea was to have fun, to lessen the seriousness.

Not everyone who was there, I daresay, agreed on the issues of sexuality facing the church. It did not matter. We had a lot of fun together. American young people and African young people worked well together as counselors. From the first moment, they were outside teaching each other the songs and games they knew from their respective childhoods to share with the campers. African teachers and American teachers consulted on their respective teaching centers. All the volunteers of diverse cultures, theologies, and experiences stood together in an assembly line washing dishes at an outside sink. There were no cross words. An American bishop notoriously scared of snakes (me!) volunteered to help hold a python and scratched the belly of a warthog. Everyone laughed out loud. Mission resulted. One of the campers told me on the last night, "We will remember about God." I think the heavens wept for joy.

I flew from South Africa to England, however, for the decennial gathering of Anglican bishops from around the world at the invitation of the Archbishop of Canterbury. Even before arriving, the atmosphere was thick with tension. Some invitees refused to come because of the others (mostly Americans and Canadians) who had been invited. The press predicted the demise of the Anglican Communion. Controversy surrounded everything. I received a frantic call from a church leader the day before I left for England about his fears for the meeting. I could feel myself getting more and more serious. It did not encourage creative thinking, and none of it sounded like the least bit of fun. Seriousness is not so conducive to relationships. The relationships have to come first. Love must precede truth, and love requires maturity. We need to be reminded that love does not insist on its own way.[17]

The third suggestion is legal. Our canons are both a blessing and a curse. They are a blessing in that they are important guarantees against the abuse of power in the church and in that they provide a framework of order in which our community can, when it works, allow us to fight out our disagreements without killing each other, as siblings should. The curse is that because they were written without contemplating the exact current situation, their overly rigid application has the unintended consequence of enforcing sameness instead of providing the room we need to work out the issues among us. The good news is that canons are amendable if there is a will to maturity.

I do not know exactly what a solution might look like, but it is possible to imagine at least a few different approaches. I am reminded of the great service done by an ambiguous canon in 1946 when the Episcopal Church was wracked by the dispute about allowing remarriage after divorce. The canons, rather than being rigid, in that case offered flexibility that allowed an honoring of admittedly inconsistent integrities until a consensus emerged, which fostered a mature approach to the problems of the day. I offer two possibilities more in the hope of stimulating creative thinking than implying an endorsement.

We might, for example, even within the context of our existing canons, create two rites within the Episcopal Church, one for traditionalists and one for progressives. The rites would allow like-thinking people to seek counsel and community together without finding it necessary to leave the church. The rites would be of temporary duration, perhaps twenty or thirty years, with the intention that purposeful work toward reconciliation take place during the duration of their existence.

A second canonical approach would be minor amendments governing what happens when clergy of the Episcopal Church wish to disassociate from the Episcopal Church and affiliate with another church of the Anglican Communion but continue to minister to congregations in the United States. I must admit that I cannot find a way to make peace with this process of foreign churches interfering in the life of the Episcopal Church within the United States and Episcopal clergy taking part in that, but I do not doubt the good faith of most of those involved. I can think of a way to amend the canons so that such individuals could find a way to leave the Episcopal Church without having to be charged under a canon with the misleading name of "Abandonment of the Communion of this Church," and that might be more likely to allow them, in time, to return with dignity.

A third approach might be to reframe the issue and deal with it accordingly. Rather than seeing the current dispute as about either orthodoxy or justice, it might be possible to see it as about pastoral care instead—how best to care pastorally for people who are, by their nature, oriented for sexual attraction to the same sex rather than the opposite sex. Once reframed, it is not difficult to imagine legislation, which might or might not be canonical, that recognizes the conflicting integrities of two inconsistent approaches to pastoral care without endorsing either, not at all unlike the 1946 canon on remarriage after divorce. Bishops would be allowed to coexist with their respective integrities for as long as necessary while the mind of the church reaches a consensus, taking as long as necessary, on the matter of same-sex relationships. I am certain that well-intended minds, particularly of canon lawyers, could find other suggestions.

A Hopeful Observation in Conclusion

There is a side chapel off the ambulatory behind the high altar at Westminster Abbey, a place dear to me as an Anglican. I find it a hopeful sign of God's intention, much like the hopeful sign I observed in two of my bishop colleagues before the vote at the 2003 General Convention. The chapel, though, speaks more obviously to eternity.

This particular chapel houses the tombs of two English monarchs, side by side. One is Mary, the Catholic queen who tried to reverse the course of the English Reformation and return the English church to obedience to Rome. The other is Elizabeth I, the Protestant queen under whom the final break with Rome took place. They lived in a time of distinct lack of clarity and extreme seriousness in matters of religion. In life, they did not see things the same way. In fact, they were as close to being diametrically opposed as two people might be. One came close to taking the life of the other. They have entered eternity together, however, as a sign of God's intention and perhaps God's sense of humor. There they lie, two powerful women, siblings, symbolizing an eternal relationship beyond the divide of death and across the divide of opinion, theology, and orthodoxy. Their marble effigies are a monument, not only to them, but to maturity, and to the civility maturity so fragilely promotes.

Notes

1. "The Archbishop of Canterbury Concluding Presidential Address to the Lambeth Conference 2008" Anglican Communion News Service, 3 August 2008 (http://www.anglicancommunion.org/acns/news.cfm/2008/8/3/ACNS4511).

2. See, e.g., John 17:11.

3. To Anglicans, the Book of Common Prayer is foundational not only to worship, but to belief. As a source of authority, it represents the weight of church tradition and would be surpassed in importance only by the Bible. The impact of revisions to it cannot be overstated.

4. Eric Gorski, "Americans change faiths at rising rate, survey finds," *AJC.com*, 25 February 2008, http://www.ajc.com/news/content/news/stories/2008/02/25/religionsurvey_0226.html.

5. Rose French, "Southern Baptist membership, baptisms decline in 2007," *ABCnews.com*, 25 April 2008, http://abc-news.go.com/US/wireStory?id=4722784.

6. *Locke v. Davey*, 540 U.S. 712 (2004).

7. *Aguilar v. Felton*, 473 U.S. 402 (1985).

8. Witness the fact, for example, that humankind has gone from the first flight at Kitty Hawk to walking on the moon within a single generation.

9. See, e.g., Stand Firm in Faith (http://www.standfirminfaith.com/); Drell's Descants (http://descant.wordpress.com/page/2/); Titus One Nine (http://www.kendallharmon.net/t19/).

10. Anglican/Roman Catholic International Commission, *The Anglican-Roman Catholic Agreement on the Eucharist*, 2nd ed. (Bramcote: Grove Books, 1972).

11. Edwin Augustine White and Jackson A. Dykman, Annotated *Constitution and Canons*, vol. 1 (Wilton CT: Morehouse-Barlow Co., 1981) 418 (emphasis added).

12. Norman Doe, *Canon Law in the Anglican Communion* (Oxford: University Press, 1998) 283 ff.

13. The principle of toleration was articulated in the Act of Uniformity of 1559, which mandated the use of the 1559 Prayer Book with its theological inconsistencies, and the principle of local autonomy was articulated in the Act of Supremacy, which declared the English monarch the supreme governor of the Church of England.

14. Genesis 18:1-15.

15. Rule of Benedict 53.

16. Christine D. Pohl, *Making Room: Recovering Hospitality as a Christian Tradition* (Grand Rapids: Eerdmans, 1999) 65.

17. 1 Corinthians 13:5.

Chapter 4

Civility and the Common Good

John Gehring and Alexia Kelley, Catholics in Alliance for the Common Good

For some, civility may seem like a quaint virtue of a bygone era before cable news shows turned into glorified shouting matches and city council meetings featured obscenity-laced tirades from angry citizens. We reminisce wistfully about a time when erudite elected officials disagreed with decorum and popular culture embodied the high-minded ideals of public enlightenment. Surely, we often romanticize the supposed genteel nature of earlier eras.

Let's not forget that in 1805, Vice President Aaron Burr and Alexander Hamilton resolved long-simmering arguments that played in and out of the pages of the day's newspapers by carrying revolvers to a hilltop overlooking the Hudson River. Hamilton died a day later from wounds inflicted in the duel.

Despite this impulse to view the past through rose-colored glasses, it is hard to deny that exemplars of civility today have become increasingly rare. Ann Coulter and Rush Limbaugh have made lucrative careers demeaning ideological opponents. Music lyrics glorify brazen violence, no-strings sexuality, and misogyny as a masculine code. Public officials attack each other not solely on the merits of ideas, but with personal animus that demonizes political opponents. Sadly, these trends sometimes even creep into spiritual and ecclesial communities that should model how words and actions can bind us together, rather than tear us apart.

In light of this reality, it is essential that our religious traditions play a leading role in renewing an ethic of civility in public life. Catholic social teaching has a long history of articulating the need for civility as a cornerstone of how faithful citizens are called to participate in democracy.

The U.S. Conference of Catholic Bishops, the organizational body representing the nation's Roman Catholic bishops, release a detailed statement before each presidential election that urges Catholic voters to recognize that the Catholic community brings a "consistent moral framework—drawn from basic human reason that is illuminated by Scripture and the teaching of the Church—for assessing issues, political platforms, and campaigns."

"Forming Consciences for Faithful Citizenship: A Call to Political Responsibility from the Catholic Bishops of the United States"[1] highlights the responsibility of Catholics and other people of faith to begin transforming a political and media culture often characterized by uncivil behavior.

> In the Catholic Tradition, responsible citizenship is a virtue, and participation in political life is a moral obligation. . . . [U]nfortunately, politics in our country often can be a contest of powerful interests, partisan attacks, sound bites, and media hype. The Church calls for a different kind of political engagement: one shaped by the moral convictions of well-formed consciences and focused on the dignity of every human being, the pursuit of the common good, and the protection of the weak and vulnerable."[2]

Prominent lay Catholics have also echoed this call. A year before the 2008 presidential elections, Thomas P. Melady, a former ambassador to the Vatican whose diplomatic career has included posts in Uganda and Burundi, decided that a bipartisan coalition of high-profile Catholics needed to speak up for civility as the guiding principle of public life. Just four years earlier, the Catholic community was splintered by debate over a handful of bishops denouncing Sen. John Kerry, a pro-choice Catholic, and publicly declaring him unfit to receive Communion. Media stories swirled with talk of "communion politics" and "wafer wars." Melady recruited Timothy J. May, a senior partner with Patton Boggs LLP and a trustee emeritus with the Catholic University of America, to help him organize a statement—"A Catholic Call to Observe Civility in Political Debate"[3]—that was endorsed by more than forty leaders including eleven former U.S. ambassadors and former chairmen of the Republican and Democratic National Committees. Prominent leaders in law, politics, and religion released the statement during a press conference at the National Press Club.

"The statement directly addresses controversies over Catholic politicians whose positions on various polarizing issues conflict or give the appearance of conflicting with Church teachings," Ambassador Melady explained. "Some voices have been shrill. The language at times has been offensive. The level of dialogue and conversation in too many instances has not met the standards that one expects in a country trying to establish worldwide standards for all democracies."[4]

"A Catholic Call to Observe Civility in Political Debate" acknowledges "deep divisions over some policy issues and recognize[s] that some who are active in political life and who differ with the Church's teachings on certain issues such as abortion, stem cell research, the death penalty, and the justification for war, air their differences in public and criticize the Church for these teachings." To address these polarizing issues in a civil manner, the statement offers several recommendations, including the following:

> As lay Catholics, we should not exhort the Church to condemn our political opponents by publicly denying them Holy Communion based on public dissent from Church teachings. An individual's fitness to receive communion is his or her personal responsibility. And it is a bishop's responsibility to set for his diocese the guidelines for administering communion.
>
> Catholic politicians who advertise their Catholicism as part of their political appeal, but ignore the Church's moral teachings in their political life confuse non-Catholics by giving the appearance of hypocrisy.
>
> Bishops, and all involved in the leadership of the Church, should not permit the Church to be used, or appear to be used, as a partisan, political tool.
>
> As Catholics, we need to keep in mind the common humanity that we share with those with whom we disagree. We must avoid seeing them as "the enemy" in a life-or-death, winner-take-all political contest.[5]

The statement goes on to describe civility as "grounded in the teachings of the Lord, who demands we love one another as we love ourselves, that we be kind, and that we forgive. From this teaching flows the command to respect even a bitter opponent, to exercise restraint in political combat, and to not use the Church for one's political purposes."

Catholics have also partnered with others in the Christian community to protect the integrity of how faith is used during the electoral process. In January 2008, Catholic and Protestant scholars, pastors, and social justice leaders came together to warn that divisive religious rhetoric from presidential candidates and relentless scrutiny of candidates' faith undermine the essential role religion can play in public life. The leaders wrote, "We are troubled to see candidates pressed to pronounce the nature of their religious beliefs, asked if they believe every word of the Bible, forced to fend off warnings by a few religious authorities about reception of sacraments, compelled to confront derogatory and false allegations of radical Muslim childhood education, and faced with prejudicial analyses of their denominational doctrines," the leaders write in the statement, "Keeping Faith: Principles to Protect Religion on the Campaign Trail."[6]

More than two dozen Catholic, evangelical, and mainline Protestant leaders called on candidates to affirm three principles to protect religion on the campaign trail: (1) avoid using religious or doctrinal differences to marginalize or disparage each other; (2) acknowledge that no single faith has an exclusive claim to moral values; and (3) recognize that policy positions should reflect the best interests of all citizens regardless of religious belief. While stressing that religion is an indispensable source of spiritual and ethical wisdom that can help us promote the common good and speak to the moral dimensions of our critical policy challenges, the leaders made a compelling case that faith should not be manipulated as a political weapon to divide voters and disparage political opponents.

Steve Schneck, a professor of political science and the director of the Life Cycle Institute at the Catholic University of America in Washington, spearheaded the idea for the statement. For Schneck, "citizens' strength of character and freedom of mind require virtues that under gird the political conditions in which they thrive."[7] These virtues include mutual respect, tolerance, and civility. However, Schneck sees civility as a quintessentially Christian virtue and has some wise thoughts about how people of faith can be both prophetic and civil.

> Some historians of ideas and political theorists make the claim that civility is a modern and liberal virtue, and try to trace its significant origin to the conclusion of the religious wars of the 16th and 17th centuries. But, I think such accounts are inadequately informed. Civility in my reading is a core Christian virtue, intimately concerned with the humility, hospitality, and gentleness that the Apostles tell us characterized the earliest Christian communities.
>
> Given that Christ was no militant and preached precisely these virtues, this is how it should be. Gospel accounts are replete with examples of Christ's own civility—eating at table with sinners and Samaritans, praising the meek, and even speaking respectfully before Pilate. Excepting only perhaps the expulsion of the moneylenders from the Temple, I think it's fair to say that even Christ's prophetic challenge to evil always proceeded from a profound and loving humility—the outward character of which might be called civility. The lesson here, though, is neither tolerance nor withdrawal

from engagement. Think, for example, of Christ's rescue of the adulteress from stoning. He did not shout at the stoners nor lambaste the sinner but neither did he tolerate. Instead, gently—with civility—he instructed and counseled "Sin no more." As Christians, we are morally obliged to speak truth to power, but how we do that must be with civility.[8]

In the Catholic social tradition, civility is a requirement for building a culture that serves the common good, a principle that stands at the center of Catholic teaching. The common good calls us to translate biblical admonitions to love our neighbors as ourselves into public policies that reflect these values in the real world. According to the *Catechism of the Catholic Church*, the common good is, in fact, "the very reason the political authority exists." A Catholic vision of the common good builds on concepts first articulated by Aristotle and later St. Thomas Aquinas, who spoke about the good sought by all as intertwined with the reality of God. Pope Leo XIII, in his 1891 encyclical *Rerum Novarum*, was the first to make formal use of the concept as the starting point for the Church's social analysis.

In the Catholic imagination, the common good is rooted in the foundational belief that all of us are created in the image of God and have inherent dignity. The intrinsic worth and sacred dignity of all people challenges Christians, in a particular way, when we face interpersonal or political disagreements around issues that have the potential to sow division and acrimony.

Catholics in Alliance for the Common Good, a nonprofit, nonpartisan organization dedicated to promoting a broader understanding of Catholic social teaching in the media and public square, convened national Catholic social justice leaders in December 2007 to challenge the strident tone of Fox news media personalities and other commentators who have aggressively lashed out at a so-called "War on Christmas" being waged by secular Americans.

The following "Open Letter to Christmas 'Culture Warriors'" ran as an advertisement in the *Washington Times, New York Post*, and *National Catholic Reporter*. The goal was to persuade influential media voices to end the Christmas "culture wars" and join people of goodwill "in a new campaign of civility and conscience that restores our focus on the common good during this holy season."[9]

The letter was signed by more than a dozen Christian leaders, professors, and writers including Reverend Randall Balmer, a professor of American Religious History at Barnard College and Columbia University; Sr. Simone

Campbell, executive director of NETWORK, a National Catholic Social Justice Lobby; and Reverend Derrick Harkins, senior pastor at the Nineteenth Street Baptist Church in Washington, D.C.

An Open Letter to Christmas "Culture Warriors"

For the past several years some media pundits and "culture warriors" have launched an aggressive campaign against a so-called "War on Christmas." Targeting department stores, local governments, and school systems for replacing Merry Christmas with "Happy Holidays" or "Seasons Greetings," Bill O'Reilly and John Gibson of Fox News have led the charge against what they call a "secular progressive agenda" determined to drive religion out of the public square. William Donohue of the Catholic League for Religious and Civil Rights ominously warns of "cultural fascists" taking over Christmas.

It's time for a ceasefire in the Christmas culture wars.

As Americans of faith, we also see a dangerous assault on the true meaning of this sacred holiday. But our outrage has little to do with a few examples of people saying "Happy Holidays" instead of "Merry Christmas." We believe the real assault on Christmas is how a season of peace, forgiveness, and goodwill has been sidelined by a focus on excessive consumerism.

The powerful message Christ brings to the world is "good news for the poor." Instead, Christmas is being reduced to a corporate-sponsored holiday that idolizes commerce and materialism. Shopping and gift giving are meaningful traditions that can express the season's values, but perspective is lost when relentless advertising and maxed-out credit cards define the holiday. It's time to reclaim the virtue of shared sacrifice for the common good.

To focus on how department stores greet customers at a time when American soldiers are dying in Iraq and 37 million of our neighbors live in poverty is a distraction from the profound moral challenges we face in confronting the real threats to human dignity in our world.

We invite Messrs. O'Reilly, Gibson, and Donohue to join us in a new campaign of civility and conscience that restores our focus on the common good during this holy season. Together we can change the culture—not with strident attacks or shouting matches on television—but with an unwavering commitment to justice and peace for all of God's children.[10]

One of the most intriguing campaigns to help unite ideological opponents around a shared vision of civility, compassion, and mutual respect is an effort organized by the Washington, D.C.-based organization Third Way. In fall 2007, the organization's Culture Program released a paper titled "Come Let Us Reason Together: A Fresh Look at Shared Cultural Values between Evangelicals and Progressives."[11] The initiative had the ambitious aim of what its authors described as ushering in "the beginning of the end of the culture wars."[12]

It is not news to anyone that for decades, issues like abortion, same-sex marriage, stem-cell research, and the role of religion in public life have been the source of sharp, often intensely bitter disagreement among Americans. While divergent views on these issues are expected, *Come Let us Reason Together* makes the case that it's possible to move beyond "the divisiveness and rancor of recent years" and to be guided by a spirit of civility and compassion. The title of the paper (from Isa 1:18) "functions as a powerful symbol of people coming together to reconcile their differences through respectful engagement."[13]

Endorsed by prominent evangelical Christians, including Reverend Joel Hunter, pastor of the 10,000-strong congregation Northland Church, and Dr. David Gushee, a professor of Christian ethics at Mercer University, the paper outlines several basic principles as initial steps in bridging longstanding divides and healing some of the "broken trust" between progressives and evangelicals. These include the following: (1) Respect for religious beliefs and religious diversity is vital for a healthy society. (2) Religion plays an appropriate public, not just private, role in American life. (3) All citizens have a constitutionally protected right to articulate the religious and moral basis of their political views in the public square, and protecting these expressions does not conflict with a commitment to non-establishment of religion.

One of the "deepest areas of disagreement" between evangelicals and progressives, the paper notes, relates to "legal rights for gay and lesbian people." While these differences are rooted in myriad theological and philosophical beliefs about homosexuality, *Come Let Us Reason Together* argues, "in the midst of real differences, there are shared principles that are rooted in respect for human dignity, and commitments to both the Golden Rule and religious liberty."[14] In regard to abortion, arguably the most divisive cultural issue of our time, the report sees opportunity for civil dialogue since "Progressives and Evangelicals can both agree that given the high number of abortions that occur every year in America, we should join together to reduce the need for abortion."[15]

In addition to these critical efforts to foster civil dialogue on hot-button issues, religious leaders are also pushing back against political smears. Since November 2005, an interfaith coalition of more than 100 pastors, priests, rabbis, and lay leaders from Roman Catholicism, two traditions of Judaism, Islam, and more than fifteen Protestant denominations have partnered to raise a powerful moral voice for the poor and marginalized in Ohio. We Believe Ohio also sponsors a statewide campaign to ensure that Ohio is a "Political Sleaze-Free Zone" where candidates for public office and elected officials are discouraged from using derogatory language or gratuitous attack ads. The coalition circulated a petition before the 2008 campaign season calling on candidates for public office to run clean, positive campaigns. For these religious leaders, political campaign tactics reflect on the quality of character and moral values candidates bring to public service. Before the campaign even began, the petition drew more than 1,000 signatures.

Press conferences were held with clergy in both Columbus and Cleveland. Gov. Ted Strickland thanked the interfaith alliance for "elevating political discourse in Ohio."[16] In a press release announcing the campaign, Rev. Dr. John Lentz of Forest Hill Presbyterian Church said that the initiative "celebrates the diversity of opinion in the state and welcomes honest debate and common disagreement. . . . It marginalizes no one. It affirms an essential commandment of all faith traditions: 'Thou shalt not bear false witness.'"[17]

While the failure of political leaders to uphold standards of decency are well chronicled, incivility and deep divisions within church communities are also not uncommon. The late cardinal Joseph Bernardin of Chicago epitomized for many Catholics a compelling model for how to heal divisions and maintain civility and mutual respect in the face of polarization.

The Second Vatican Council, more commonly known as Vatican II, was a series of historic meetings held in Rome from 1962 to 1965. Pope John XXIII had opened the windows of the Church to the modern world, and the ensuing reforms reverberated throughout Christendom. The array of liturgical reforms and statements on ecumenical and interfaith relations changed the public face of the Catholic Church. It also ignited a sharp debate among priests, laity, and Catholic theologians about the future of Catholicism. In the decades following Vatican II, Cardinal Bernardin and others lamented the growing ideological and political divisions within the Church as liberal and conservative factions tussled over finding a proper balance between preserving tradition and modernizing reforms. In an effort to address this polarization, Bernardin inaugurated the Catholic Common Ground Initiative in 1996 with the release of a statement, "Called to Be Catholic: Church in a Time of Peril."

"Called to Be Catholic," prepared by the National Pastoral Life Center, was a frank assessment. It described the Catholic Church facing a "time of peril" because of diminished numbers of Catholics attending Mass, demoralized clergy, and intense debates over the impact of Vatican II. In order to address this mood of "suspicion and acrimony," the statement acknowledged the benefits of constructive debate and disagreement while also challenging lay Catholics and church leaders to "approach the Church's current situation with fresh eyes, open minds, and changed hearts" and to pursue "disagreements in a renewed spirit of dialogue." Specifically, the report urged Catholics to be guided by civility as outlined in the following principles.

- We should recognize that no single group or viewpoint in the Church has a complete monopoly on the truth.
- We should presume that those with whom we differ are acting in good faith. They deserve civility, charity, and a good-faith effort to understand their concerns.
- We should be cautious in ascribing motives. We should not impugn another's love of the Church and loyalty to it.
- We should not rush to interpret disagreements as conflicts of starkly opposing principles rather than as differences in degree or in prudential pastoral judgments about the relevant facts.[18]

This commitment to genuine engagement and finding common ground across the divides of political agendas or ideology should serve as an animating principle for people of faith in a pluralistic society. It requires a spirit of humility that acknowledges that pursuit of truth is always imperfect and exposure to opposing perspectives enriches our understanding. Seeking authentic dialogue on shared principles does not mean abandoning core beliefs or papering over disagreements.

Let's consider an example of how a charged social issue—the right of gays and lesbians to marry—played out during a high-profile state ballot initiative in California. In November 2008, California's Proposition 8 proposal to amend the state constitution to restrict the definition of marriage as a union between a man and a woman attracted national media attention and more than $70 million in combined campaign advocacy expenses. Fifty-two percent of voters approved the ban on gay marriage.

In the following days, thousands of protesters marched in California denouncing the vote, several Mormon churches were vandalized (the Mormon Church spent millions of dollars lobbying for the proposal), and

Catholic bishops in California faced sharp public criticism for endorsing Proposition 8.

Both sides on this polarizing issue felt misunderstood. Gays and lesbians saw themselves as targets of injustice. Religious leaders felt demonized for upholding traditional Christian views about marriage. In the wake of this ballot initiative, the Catholic archbishop of San Francisco, George H. Niederauer, offered a plea for dialogue and civility in *Catholic San Francisco*, the newspaper of the Archdiocese of San Francisco. "Tolerance, respect, and trust are always two-way streets, and tolerance, respect, and trust do not include agreement, or even approval," the archbishop wrote in his open letter. He continued,

> We need to be able to disagree without being disagreeable. We need to stop talking as if we are experts on the real motives of people with whom we have never spoken. We need to stop hurling names like "bigot" and "pervert" at each other. And we need to stop it now. For our part, we churchgoers need to speak and act out of the truth that all people are God's children and unconditionally loved by God.[19]

While these words alone are unlikely to heal wrenching divisions and feelings of mistrust and anger on both sides, they do offer the potential for the beginning of a new dialogue rooted in civility and compassion on this and other difficult social issues.

Practicing Civility: Recapturing a Lost Art

Anyone who has competed on a college or high school debate team learned the rules of civil debate and argument. Unlike today's politics and shouting-match talk shows, the victors in competitive debates were determined on the merits of their arguments, the soundness of their positions, and the level of rhetorical skills. Whatever happened to civil and substantive argument, the kind that used to prevail even between deeply opposed political rivals? Or to the belief that engaging in civil debate regarding bold and passionately felt differences could be constructive and fruitful, leading to more innovative solutions than either side could have reached on its own?

In recent years, the practice of civil debate—a cornerstone of our democracy and a requirement of the common good—has been replaced by the practice of personal and political destruction. These vicious and disparaging tactics distract us from the substantive differences among opposing points of view and different philosophical assumptions or policy positions they reflect. The politics of destruction opt to attack the messenger of a contrary opinion instead of intelligently and politely challenging the merits of a policy position or argument. Destruction seeks not to disassemble the debater's ideas but rather to annihilate his or her character, credibility, or personality.[20]

The Bush administration mounted a classic campaign of personal destruction when it collected intelligence to justify going to war in Iraq. As part of related intelligence gathering, the Central Intelligence Agency sent a former U.S. ambassador Joseph Wilson to Niger to investigate reports that Iraq had sought to buy uranium there for use in weapons of mass destruction. Wilson found no evidence to support this claim, but President Bush still chose to use it to bolster his case for going to war. When Wilson later challenged the administration in a 2003 *New York Times* opinion piece, a campaign of personal destruction began.

Rather than disputing Wilson's argument or the evidence, the White House attacked Wilson's credibility. As part of that process, it used the media to reveal that Wilson's wife, Valerie Plame, was a CIA operative. Because Plame may have been involved in facilitating her husband's mission, the White House suggested, Wilson's findings were invalid. In effect, the administration destroyed a messenger who advanced an honest but unfavorable argument, showing little regard for the implications of national security, the safety of Plame's sources, and the integrity of the CIA. In a well-publicized legal case, *United States v. Libby*, White House official Lewis "Scooter" Libby took the fall for the administration's leak of Plame's identity. The politics of destruction claimed victory over civil argument and hard evidence.[21]

Civility is essential to the kinds of constructive debate and honest deliberations that fortify any functional democracy. Democracy is built on the understanding that there are indeed differences among people, values, and political approaches. But it also holds that through civil deliberation and rational argument, we can discuss these differences and forge new solutions based on respect for all views and engagement with all parties. Civility and respect are integral to our marriages and personal relationships as well. We all know from experience that when disrespect, scorn, or abuse toward another person become the norm in a family or a marriage, it is hard to find peace or any practical solutions. Civility is a Christian practice. It flows from the essential belief that we are created in God's image and are therefore worthy of respect and decent treatment from our fellow human beings.

Though we may disagree, even passionately, on numerous matters, we should never seek to denigrate someone's character or integrity. We challenge their opinions or arguments, not their very being. Civility should not be seen as a muzzle that stifles us from expressing and fighting for our deeply held convictions. Nor is it a harness that should restrict us from fighting back when our position or character is challenged or even attacked by others. When we do fight back and stand up for our convictions, we should always seek the high ground and answer these challenges and personal attacks in a spirit of civility.

Older members of Congress often reminisce about the days when legislators from both sides of the aisle met for drinks or social dinners after work. These occasions helped politicians of vastly different stripes cultivate bonds of friendship and mutual respect that set the tone for more constructive debate and negotiations during long days of legislating. Sometimes creative give-and-take solutions or breakthrough compromises were forged over late-night dinners or card games where civility and trust developed despite political and ideological differences. Republican President Ronald Reagan and Democratic Speaker of the House "Tip" O'Neill hammered out a compromise that improved Social Security.

Today, Justices Ruth Bader Ginsburg and Antonin Scalia, ideological opponents on the Supreme Court, cultivate a friendship outside the Court by attending opera performances together and sharing a strong commitment to their families. This kind of civility has helped our government get things done despite strong differences of opinion or approach.[22]

The common good suffers when we refuse even to participate in dialogue, when we fail to discuss our differences, or when a "my way or the highway" approach leads us to disengage. We have seen the practice of disengagement ruin our political process and erode the common good, and we have seen it ruin marriages and communities. In politics, when deeply divided adversaries disengage from dialogue with each other, progress on important issues can grind to a halt.

The abortion debate serves as an excellent example of what happens when disengagement triumphs over compromise. The conversation has become so polarized that social, economic, and cultural efforts to reduce abortion—efforts widely supported by most Americans—often are pushed to the margins. For decades, those on opposing sides of this issue have hurled angry rhetoric at each other from entrenched positions and refused to find common ground. Fortunately, this debate is slowly changing as pro-life and pro-choice elected officials are beginning to unite behind comprehensive abortion reduction strategies that address the socioeconomic factors that often drive women to make this tragic choice.

This does not mean that those who view abortion as an evil and those who see it as a woman's reproductive right relinquish their core convictions. It means common ground and good-faith dialogue is possible—in fact essential—even amid deeply opposed positions. Democracy is about the "art of the possible," and without constructive, civil exchanges there is little hope for progress.

Civility and Conviction

One of the troubling defining characteristics of our current political culture is that citizens are often presented with a collection of false choices— national security *or* civil liberties, a strong economy *or* a thriving natural environment. These either/or choices mistakenly convince us that we cannot hope to build a society for the common good without giving up on our individual success. Indeed, false choices obscure a set of real choices that requires vigorous conversation, civility, and compromise. These virtues do not compete with the virtue of conviction but indeed require it.

Why don't enough of our leaders speak from their hearts about who they are and what they believe? In many ways, it is because they are afraid of losing elections and speaking uncomfortable truths that do not test well with polling. Sen. Robert Casey, Jr., of Pennsylvania recognized this temptation when he ran for the Senate in 2006 in a state deeply divided between pro-life and pro-choice constituencies. Casey took the issue head on: "You can't have it both ways and say, 'I am pro-choice but . . ." or 'I am pro-life but . . . ,'" he said of his own position on abortion.[23] In this way, Casey cut through the politics of division and found a way to appeal to both pro-life and pro-choice voters.

He accomplished this not by speaking from both sides of his mouth but by finding common ground and focusing on root causes of abortion (lack of health care and economic support for women and families) instead of the lightning rod of whether or not abortion should be legal. Voters responded, choosing Democrat Casey over Catholic Republican Rick Santorum, in part because Casey's beliefs—his convictions—were clear and meshed with his political views.[24]

We are blessed with other public officials who embrace conviction over fear. Even though Republican Senator Chuck Hagel of Nebraska voted to authorize the Iraq war, he called for an end to the war when it became apparent that the invasion was not achieving our foreign policy objectives in the region. Despite the fact that this could have hurt him politically, Hagel made his case both with civility and conviction.

Democrat Tim Kaine won the 2005 Virginia governor's race, campaigning as an ardent foe of the death penalty. When opposition attack ads claimed he believed "Adolf Hitler doesn't qualify for the death penalty," Kaine refused to lash out in anger and stuck to his convictions, citing his Catholic faith's teaching that all life is sacred. Republican Senator Olympia Snowe of Maine has also taken unpopular stands within her party on several occasions, opposing the size of President Bush's 2003 tax cuts, for example, and challenging the administration's handling of the Iraq war. In 2005, she participated in the bipartisan "Gang of 14" compromise, which ended a contentious impasse over Supreme Court nominations.

Tom Perriello, a newly elected member of Congress representing Virginia's 5th District, decided to run for office after years of being a leader in various faith and global justice organizations. A co-founder of Catholics in Alliance for the Common Good, Perriello was inspired by a vision that a new "politics of conviction" was essential for renewing the ideal of public life as public service. Perriello, thirty-four, faced an improbable victory against incumbent Rep. Virgil Goode, who ran a number of negative ads against the first-time candidate. Despite the attack ads and mudslinging, Perriello never veered from his principled message of transcending partisanship and serving the common good. In one of the biggest upsets of the 2008 campaign, Perriello defeated Goode. In an e-mail to supporters, Congressman-elect Perriello explained his positive, civil approach to politics. "What we wanted to offer was a people-powered, principled, problem-solving campaign that was not about tearing apart the other side, but rather about leaving behind a failed approach to politics from both sides," he wrote.

The erosion of civility in politics also extends to a consumerist popular culture. Vincent Miller, a professor of theology at Georgetown University and author of *Consuming Religion: Christian Faith and Practice in Consumer Culture*, offers an incisive perspective on how commercialization and making an idol of "choice" impacts notions of civility.[25]

> When we think of consumer culture, we think too quickly of greed and materialism. Its most profound effects happen long before questions of morality arise. This is true in regard to its impact upon civility as well. No

doubt there is an abundance of greed and materialism and this is certainly corrosive of civility.

Consumer culture's more subtle workings are, however, much more destructive of civility. Market exchange is a social practice that forms our character in a profound way. Such exchanges are revealed in their purest form on the Internet: consider goods, choose and pay with a click, receive. While commerce in its original meanings involved interaction with others (thus its sexual and conversational meanings), it has been refined in our day into a mere exercise of will in relation to things. As a result, we never learn the skills of engaging and negotiating with others. We're uncomfortable receiving a sales pitch or disagreeing on a choice. We prefer the silence of things and the compliance of checkout clerks. Alas, politics requires more substantial interactions. It is a preeminently social process of proposals and debate, coalition building, and policy refinement. It is utterly predictable that in a consumer culture, politics would likely be reduced to a matter of incommensurable choices between positions that do not dialogue with one another, and that political power would be conceived as a winner-take-all exercise or one of obstructionism.[26]

Cardinal Theodore McCarrick, the retired archbishop of Washington, D.C., has long been concerned with the coarsening of our nation's political culture and believes as Miller does that churches should be in the vanguard of a new movement for civility in public life. In June 2006, he delivered a speech—"Restoring Civility to Political Discourse"[27]—before a gathering of Catholic members of Congress. His words are worthy of close examination.

I urge you to restore greater civility to the political discourse of our country. Many of you have been the targets of attack ads and vitriolic political speech. Even as a bishop, I have experienced similar public attacks. One example: A group—this one was on the right, but it could have been on the left—took out a full-page ad to condemn me because I would not deny Communion to some Catholic public officials.

Then they placed an ad attacking all the bishops for our refusal to do the same. Then they ran an ad calling for Pope John Paul II to remove me and then-Cardinal Ratzinger for our lack of fidelity to their particular vision of faith. . . . We need robust and principled debate on the difficult issues of our day. But we must break out of the war-room tactics, the daily recriminations, the impugning of motives. We could start with, "Thou shall not bear false witness."

We have to build bridges to common sense in pursuit of the common good, even when this requires crossing partisan and ideological divisions.

Would it be naïve to ask why Catholic political leaders could not take the lead in rejecting the politics of polarization? We must restore civility to public discourse so that we attack problems and not one another.

McCarrick's call to build bridges and pursue the common good across ideological divisions challenges people of faith to become models of prudence and civility. In an increasingly fragmented age where interest groups work on narrow agendas, the tenor of public debate is shrill, and politics has become characterized by hyper-partisanship, faithful citizens should model a different example that puts the principles of integrity and civility at the core of our private and public lives.

Notes

1. "Forming Consciences for Faithful Citizenship: A Call to Political Responsibility from the Catholic Bishops of the United States," November 2007, http://www.usccb.org/faithfulcitizenship/FCStatement.pdf. See also FaithfulCitizenship.org.

2. "Forming Consciences for Faithful Citizenship," 9.

3. "A Catholic Call to Observe Civility in Political Debate," Catholics in Alliance for the Common Good, 6 November 2007, http://www.catholicsinalliance.org/node/18609.

4. "Prominent Catholics Call For Civility in Politics," Catholics in Alliance for the Common Good, 6 November 2007, http://www.catholicsinalliance.org/node/18609.

5. "A Catholic Call to Observe Civility in Political Debate."

6. "Keeping Faith: Principles to Protect Religion on the Campaign Trail,"
Catholics in Alliance for the Common Good, 16 January 2008, http://www.catholicsinalliance.org/node/18547.

7. Steve Schneck, personal communication with John Gehring.

8. Ibid.

9. "An Open Letter to Christmas 'Culture Warriors,'" Catholics in Alliance for the Common Good, 12 December 2007, http://www.catholicsinalliance.org/node/18456.

10. Ibid.

11. Rachel Laser, Robert Jones, et al., "Come Let Us Reason Together: A Fresh Look at Shared Cultural Values between Evangelicals and Progressives," Third Way Culture Program, October 2007, http://www.thirdway.org/data/product/file/107/Come_Let_Us_Reason_Together_Report.pdf.

12. Third Way, "Progressives, Evangelical Leaders Seek 'End of the Culture Wars,'" news release, 10 October 2007.

13. Laser and Jones, et al., "Come Let Us Reason Together," 5.

14. Ibid., 24.

15. Ibid., 25.

16. We Believe Ohio, "Clergy Declare Ohio a 'Political Sleaze-Free Zone,'" press release, 8 November 2007.

17. Ibid.

18. "Called to Be Catholic: Church in a Time of Peril," National Pastoral Life Center, Catholic Common Ground Initiative, 1996, http://www.nplc.org/commonground/calledcatholic.htm.

19. "Open Letter from Archbishop George H. Niederauer," *Catholic San Francisco*, 5 December 2008.

20. Alexia Kelley and Chris Korzen, *A Nation for All: How the Catholic Vision for the Common Good Can Save America from the Politics of Division* (Boston: Jossey Bass, 2008), 112.

21. Ibid., 113.

22. Ibid., 114.

23. Carrie Budoff, "Casey's clear view on abortion could muddy campaign waters," *Philadelphia Inquirer*, 18 December 2005

24. Kelley and Korzen, *A Nation for All*, 110.

25. Vincent J. Miller, *Consuming Religion: Christian Faith and Practice in Consumer Culture* (New York: Continuum, 2004).

26. Ibid.

27. Theodore McCarrick, "Restoring Civility to Political Discourse," *America: The National Catholic Weekly*, 25 September 2006, http://www.americamagazine.org/content/article.cfm?article_id=4975.

Chapter 5

Holy Conferencing

Sally Dyck,
United Methodist Church
Resident Bishop of Minnesota

The Relationship between Civility and Holy Conferencing

In the United Methodist Church, the term "holy conferencing" has emerged as a way of calling people to Christian civility from a biblical basis and from the historical precedent given by John Wesley, the founder of Methodism in the eighteenth century. Like many Christian denominations around the country and world, the United Methodist Church has found itself in intense and often heated conversations about such matters as sexuality, especially abortion and homosexuality.

However, as a denomination and local congregations, we, like other Christians, erupt into uncivil and unchristian conflict over all kinds of decisions and differences in addition to matters of sexuality. Increasingly with cell phones, e-mail, and instant messaging, communications are rapid and don't always bring out the best in us. When there is a disagreement within the life of a local church, e-mails have tarnished the reputation of the church, not to mention its pastor or a layperson. For years a church may wonder why people don't want to attend or why it isn't growing, forgetting the ways in which its members have talked about the conflict within their church to others and how relationships have been damaged in the process.

Within the denomination or even a local church, people who agree with each other tend to talk to each other only in silos. Within silos, inflammatory language emerges because there isn't a diverse body involved in the conversation. Thus, inflammatory language becomes accepted, unchallenged, and unnoticed. Yet when people begin to speak with others who disagree with them, inflammatory language becomes a major obstacle.

Outside of the denominations, independently funded organizations that wish to "purify" or "take back" the church as they envision it exist with little accountability in how they use inflammatory language. While the denominations have policies about the use of church directories, these organizations amass extensive e-mail lists to use in their efforts to tear down the body instead of build it up. They tarnish the witness of the church as they sow seeds of mistrust, fear, and misinformation. Sometimes these attacks are made on persons in leadership, demonizing them instead of clarifying how someone might actually come to another perspective from a position of faith.

Some argue that the controversial issues, such as matters of sexuality or other social justice concerns, are causing decline in membership for mainline denominations, but I would suggest that it's the *way* in which we talk to and about each other that results in decline. When we devolve into what could only be described as *unholy* conversation, we are lacking in civility as well as spiritual maturity.

Stephen L. Carter defines civility as

> the sum of the many sacrifices we are called to make for the sake of living together. When we pretend that we travel alone, we can also pretend that these sacrifices are unnecessary. . . . Rules of civility are thus also rules of morality: it is morally proper to treat our fellow citizens with respect, and morally improper not to. Our crisis of civility, then, is part of a larger crisis of morality. And because morality is what distinguishes human from other animals, the crisis is ultimately one of humanity.[1]

If civility is an issue of morality, then how we converse and relate to each other should be something that we as Christians—or for that matter, anyone of faith—regard as fundamental to who we are and how we live out our faith commitment.

Therefore, holy conferencing has emerged in the United Methodist Church as a way of reminding us that we are set apart, different from the rest of culture as Christians, and rooted in Christian practices of speech and behavior. The tacit premise of holy conferencing is that *how* we talk to and about each other in the midst of our differences is as important as the results or decisions that come from our conversations. Because when we resolve one difference or make a decision, there will always be another to resolve. Therefore we must learn how to talk to and about each other in the midst of these differences. Furthermore, holy conferencing is not meant to be a practice that we employ to save the church; it's a practice that we learn and use in all aspects of our lives and in all relationships so as to be peacemakers who follow Jesus.

The Biblical and Historical Roots of Holy Conferencing

Conferencing began with John Wesley in an official way in London in November 1739 when he and other Methodist preachers came together to discuss theological and doctrinal issues, to pray, to worship, to provide support to each other in what were often difficult and even hostile environments of ministry, and to give account of one's soul. Since then conferencing has been a major component of United Methodist tradition, history, and organization.

The term "holy conferencing" is not found in John Wesley's works anywhere, and none of us are quite sure where its usage began or who started its usage as it is now understood. But Wesley did use the term "Christian conferencing" and designated it as an instituted means of grace. Through the means of grace—prayer, Scripture reading, corporate worship, participation in the Lord's Supper, fasting and Christian conferencing—we place ourselves in a position to be available to receive God's grace in our lives.

John Wesley identified Christian conferencing as a means of grace because it positioned us so as to grow in our faith and spiritual maturity. We both learn from each other and learn to love one another in the process. It's both informational and formational in our faith. Wesley describes Christian conferencing as a means of grace by saying,

> Christian conference: Are you convinced how important and how difficult it is to "order your conversation right?" Is it "always in grace? Seasoned with salt? Meet to minister grace to the hearers?" Do not you converse too long at a time? Is not an hour commonly enough? Would it not be well always to have a determinate end in view; and to pray before and after it?[2]

"Ordering our conversations right" is an important aspect of how he understood Christian conferencing. Our speech is meant to be filled with grace, not animosity, and as a means of delivering good news or edification to others. What does Wesley's phrase "seasoned with salt" mean except that our conversations bring out the best in ourselves and in each other? Christian conferencing as a means of grace is the building up of the body of Christ, not tearing it down.

Wesley's words about "ordering our conversations right" also suggest that there are ways to format such conversations with time limitations or expectations that are clear about their outcome. Will there be a decision made? Will it come from consensus or vote? Certainly prayer—voiced and/or silent prayer—are important in holding such conversations. Prayer as well as self-control, or self-sacrifice as Stephen L. Carter stated in his definition of civility, is essential to "order our conversation" and make it holy.

As the term has changed to *holy* conferencing, it suggests that we as Christians are called to be set apart, to be different, and to become more like Christ in all aspects of our lives, including the speech which flows from our hearts. Holy conferencing is a means of grace that helps us to grow in our faith and spiritual maturity because it causes us to grow in our love of God and others. We can be impassioned about our convictions, but we also must be compassionate toward others as we express them and relate to those who differ from us.

United Methodists do a lot of conferencing. In our local churches, we have a charge or church conference that is like an annual business meeting for the church. Members are invited to come and make decisions about the upcoming year's budget, goals, and direction. We also have annual conferences that are the equivalent of a diocese or regional area, and each has an episcopal leader. These meetings happen, as they would suggest, on a yearly and regional basis. During them, attendees make similar decisions plus commission and ordain new clergy.

We also have jurisdictional conferences that include larger regional areas (there are five in the United States) that meet every four years, and among the business at them, bishops are elected. Every four years, prior to the jurisdictional conferences, a General Conference makes decisions for the whole worldwide denomination. The General Conference is the only body that can speak for the whole denomination. So as United Methodists, we do a lot of conferencing!

All of these conferences grew out of John Wesley's first desire for people, clergy and laity, to come together for education, fellowship, worship, prayer, theological discussion, and mutual accountability in the Christian faith. Small groups, known as class meetings and bands, were a significant part of the discipleship building of the early Methodist movement in the United States. These small groups were where Methodists learned to conference or converse with each other about the state of their souls. Again, they were informational and formational in the faith and still play a central role in Methodism's method of encouraging spiritual maturity. Since Christianity is meant to be lived in community and not in isolation, through small groups and conferencing, we "move toward perfection in love" which was John Wesley's way of saying that we are called to grow in our love toward God *and* others.

The surprising realization for many United Methodist Christians is that John Wesley regarded these conferences as a means of grace! Too often in our modern experience, they seem anything but grace-filled. Or people don't invest themselves in small groups or see conferencing as a way to grow in faith. Conferencing seems a bit of a stretch to the imagination when United Methodist Christians, like many others, set themselves against each other in word and action, emphasizing our differences rather than our common ground of faith.

To conference means to come together to "con-fer," or mutually search for truth. Some United Methodists resist this definition, saying that the Bible tells us what is truth and it's simply our job to respond to that truth. If it were as easy as that, I don't think we'd find ourselves in the contentious and divisive conversations, not to mention experiencing broken relationships and a church threatened at times with schism. A major obstacle to holy conferencing is when any one body—individual or group—claims to have the corner on truth and leaves no room for conferring or mutually searching for truth. Truth may be greater than an answer; truth may in fact be the relationship that exists in seeking the answer.

Parker Palmer has said,

> Truth is an eternal conversation about things that matter, conducted with passion and discipline. It's not the outcomes of the conversation that matter because the outcomes keep changing. It's the conversation of the community itself. And if I want my students to be in the truth, I want them to know how to be in the conversation, not just resting in the conclusions. I want them to know how to hang in with a conversation that's increasingly difficult because it's increasingly diverse and it involved much woundedness, and much anger and much struggle. There are ways to stay in the conversation if you understand that that's what truth is.[3]

I've carried this quote around on a bright yellow piece of paper for many years. This is my hope for the United Methodist Church as I serve it. These difficult and diverse conversations don't just exist in the church. They exist in our lives at work, school, home, family, and other organizations to which we belong. And when one difficult conversation is over, there will be yet another difficult conversation to have. The greatest gift that the church can give people is an opportunity to learn how to holy conference, not to save the church, but to bring peace into our lives on an individual, community, and even world level.

But Methodism didn't invent Christian conferencing, nor did we start conflict and controversy in the church! The early church became more diverse as more and more people were included with differing ethnic backgrounds, cultures, and experiences even of the risen Christ. Creating a homogenous community isn't the example that Paul gives us in the Scriptures, particularly in 1 Corinthians 12 or Romans 12 where he speaks of the body of Christ as being diverse and needing every part or member of it. Homogeneity is not our goal; loving one another is. The early church led the way in recognizing the conflicts that such differences created and giving us examples of what could be called holy conferencing.

One of the biggest controversies in the early church can be found in Acts 15, which centers on the question of whether a Gentile needed to be circumcised (and therefore become Jewish) in order to become a Christian. Deeply held but diverse convictions gripped the early church, and they were based on Scripture and tradition. The matter heated up to the point where it could no longer be dealt with via the postal system of the day (proving that instant messaging may not be the only source of conflict) but necessitated a face-to-face meeting of the various perspectives.

There was much debate, it says in Acts 15:6b, but the whole assembly also listened and sat in silence as they reflected upon the passionate speeches given. Peter—upon whom Jesus built the church and who claimed that he was the one God chose to deliver the message to the Gentiles (Acts 15:7)—and Paul—the early church's missionary to the Gentiles and a major interpreter of the faith—were prominent thinkers and speakers on the matter. The speeches of those who disagreed—and they must have disagreed passionately—aren't included, but passion and deep conviction were a part of this Christian conferencing.

Notice that after hearing speeches, there was no voting, no Robert's Rules of Order, therefore no winners and losers based on majority vote. Notice that there was silence: presumably discernment. Notice that James—the leader—discerned a way forward that the others then agreed to follow: a method of consensus. It was decided that "we should not trouble those Gentiles who are turning to God" (Acts 15:19). There was a gracious inclusion of the Gentiles, but conditions were given to be mindful of those who were struggling with the resolution. In other words, a compromise was met, minimizing winners and losers and recognizing the complexity of the truth of the matter.

The process used to communicate and interpret this decision is also notable. A pastoral letter was written and sent to Antioch, which had asked for a declaratory decision on the matter. In addition to a letter, a person named Judas, called Barsabbas, and one named Silas were sent along with the letter as interpreters (Acts 15:27).

Judas and Silas went to Antioch and read the letter to those waiting to hear the decision, and their human presence helped communicate its message. The congregation rejoiced at its reading and what Judas and Silas said about the process and the outcome of the conference in Jerusalem. After "encouraging and strengthening" the congregation for a while, they were "sent off in peace by the believers to those who had sent them" (Acts 15:34b). The Antioch congregation is known as being the first place where the term *Christian* was used for the followers of Jesus, but perhaps it's also the first place where Christian conferencing initiated and received the resolution of a difficult and controversial matter in the people's Christian life together.

A final resolution did not, however, put the whole thing to rest (as is often the case today). As soon as the decision was made, it appears that people began to waiver in their commitment to it. In the epistle to the Galatians, it appears from Paul's perspective that the circumcisers in Galatia tried to upset people on this issue again. This underscores the reality that such important, theological, and personal matters aren't quickly or easily put to rest.

Paul writes rather sharp words about the "circumcision party," calling them a derogatory term, *dogs*, in Philippians 3:2. He attacks Peter personally in Galatians 1:11-14, accusing him and others of being hypocrites since they were "not acting consistently with the truth of the gospel." Some have argued that Paul is speaking his truth, but I think he is using inflammatory language.

I don't raise this point to criticize Paul but to show that all of us are guilty at some point or another of inflammatory language and unholy conferencing. Paul also recognizes that there is "a more excellent way" (1 Cor 12:31b) in how we relate to each other. Love doesn't use inflammatory language, and doesn't insist on one's own way and having the sole corner on truth so as to keep from listening to others. Paul makes it clear that how we relate to each other is as important as the decisions we come to when he says, "if I have all faith, so as to remove mountains, but do not have love, I am nothing" (1 Cor 13:2b).

John Wesley wasn't a stranger to confrontational conversations either. He, too, had sharp words to say to and about others. But he wanted his detractors to stay at the table with him, saying,

> Are you persuaded you see more clearly than me? It is not unlikely that you may. Then treat me as you would desire to be treated yourself upon a change of circumstances. . . . But be not displeased if I entreat you not to beat me down in order to quicken my pace (in coming to your persuasion) . . . not to give me hard names in order to bring me into the right way. Suppose I was ever so much in the wrong, I doubt this would not set me right. Rather, it would make me run so much farther from you and so get more and more out of the way. . . . For God's sake, if it be possible to avoid it, let us not provoke one another to wrath. Let us not kindle in each other this fire of hell, much less blow it into a flame . . . if we die without love, what will knowledge avail?[4]

Wesley clearly recognizes the ineffectiveness of inflammatory, derogatory, and angry language as well as its incongruence with the gospel. His aim was that we would "not provoke one another to wrath" but build up the body of Christ through our love for one another and God.

Emergence and Practice of Holy Conferencing in the United Methodist Church

Following both the General Conferences in 2000 in Cleveland, Ohio, and 2004 in Pittsburgh, Pennsylvania, the whole denomination exemplified a weariness and fragility that affected its life and witness. In hope of averting angry and ugly confrontations at the General Conference in May 2008 in Fort Worth, Texas, the Council of Bishops and the General Conference organizers endorsed and promoted *Guidelines for Holy Conferencing—What God Expects of Us* as a blueprint for conversation as United Methodists prepared for the conferencing and as the delegates mutually searched for truth at the conference.

There was precedence for using guidelines, coming out of the *Book of Discipline.*[5] In the 1904 edition, the *Book of Discipline* emphasizes the importance of unity as Christians and what practices make for unity.

> In order to form a closer union with each other: 1. Let us be deeply convinced of the absolute necessity of it, 2. Pray earnestly for, and speak freely

to, each other, 3. When we meet, let us never part without prayer, 4. Take great care not to despise each other's gifts, 5. Never speak lightly of each other, 6. Let us defend each other's character in everything as far as it is consistent with truth, 7. Labor to honor each to prefer the other before himself.[6]

Throughout the history of the United Methodist Church, we have dealt with weighty matters that have caused schism, such as slavery in 1844, and in the early part of the twentieth century, conversations began that brought the Methodist Episcopal Church and Methodist Episcopal Church, South, back together again. The words "in order to form a closer union with each other" are not used lightly, as these deep historical divisions were brought together again in Christian community.

In the late 1990s, the United Methodist Church engaged in conversations nationally about homosexuality. "Guidelines for Civility" were developed at the time by one of the commissions. They were utilized for a purpose and then largely forgotten. Then the Young People's Assembly in Johannesburg, South Africa, in January 2007 resurrected the "Guidelines for Civility," and they became the basis for what was further adapted by the Council of Bishops and the General Commission on General Conference for the 2008 conference, producing what was called *The Guidelines for Holy Conferencing—What God Expects of Us,* based on Colossians 3:12-16a, 17.

Guidelines for Holy Conferencing—What God Expects of Us

As God's chosen ones, holy and beloved, clothe yourselves with compassion, kindness, humility, meekness, and patience. Bear with one another and, if anyone has a complaint against another, forgive each other; just as the Lord has forgiven you, so you also must forgive. Above all, clothe yourselves with love, which binds everything together in perfect harmony. And let the peace of Christ rule in your hearts, to which indeed you were called in the one body. And be thankful. Let the word of Christ dwell in you richly. . . . And whatever you do, in word or deed, do everything in the name of the Lord Jesus, giving thanks to God the Father through him. (Col 3:12-16a, 17)

- Every person is a child of God. Always speak respectfully. One can disagree without being disagreeable.
- As you patiently listen and observe the behavior of others, be open to the possibility that God can change the views of any or all parties in the discussion.
- Listen patiently before formulating responses.

- Strive to understand the experience out of which others have arrived at their views.
- Be careful in how you express personal offense at differing opinions. Otherwise dialogue may be inhibited.
- Accurately reflect the views of others when speaking. This is especially important when you disagree with that position.
- Avoid using inflammatory words, derogatory names, or an excited and angry voice.
- Avoid making generalizations about individuals and groups. Make your point with specific evidence and examples.
- Make use of facilitators and mediators.
- Remember that people are defined, ultimately, by their relationship with God—not by the flaws we discover, or think we discover, in their views and actions.
- We believe Christians can discuss important issues without the acrimonious debate and parliamentary maneuvering that can divide a group into contending factions. We see too many examples of that in secular society. We believe the Holy Spirit leads in all things, especially as we make decisions. We want to avoid making decisions in a fashion that leaves some feeling like winners and others like losers. We can change the world through honest conversation on matters about which we are passionate.

Guidelines for Holy Conferencing—What God Expects from Us was shared throughout the denomination prior to General Conference 2008. Holy conferencing was widely discussed prior to the conference, and a general commitment prevailed in keeping them. The guidelines were printed in the delegates' handbook and referred to by those presiding over legislative groups and the plenary sessions. "I saw it at work," a young adult said to me one day. But it wasn't easy as discussion ensued in legislative groups or on the plenary floor. "It was hard for me to keep the guidelines when it came time to really discuss some of these issues," another young advocate for them confessed to me. There were also violations of them by all parties, and yet the guidelines generally "seasoned" the conversations and the tone of the General Conference in a positive way.

There were detractors to the guidelines and the concept of holy conferencing. In an unsigned "white paper" sent out to delegates prior to the General Conference, among the concerns was a resistance to refraining from the use of "inflammatory words, derogatory names, or an excited and angry voice." The "white paper" stated that it is "still important to allow for passionate expression of opinion." This is a common misunderstanding about holy conferencing. Holy conferencing is more than "making nice." The authors of the "white paper" were dubious about holy conferencing because they felt that the guidelines and emphasis on how we talk to and about each other were meant to keep us from talking about the deeply held convictions that undergird our controversies. Avoiding difficult topics is not holy conferencing. Avoiding crucial conversation is just as destructive as conversation laden with inflammatory language. Holy conferencing is engaging others in conversation with speech that builds up, not tears down.

Shortly before the 2008 General Conference, Senator Barack Obama, still in the primary race for the Democratic nomination for president, gave a speech on race in America that was a powerful and electrifying moment in oratorical history.[7] Senator Obama's speech provided an example of what holy conferencing is and what it is not. He demonstrated that we must *not* avoid or suppress conversation about sensitive and divisive issues. His speech was also a good demonstration of how passion and conviction can come together without being inflammatory, derogatory, or angry. He addressed a hot-button issue that most Americans can't talk about in cordial environments, much less in a context with high stakes for a presidential campaign. Surely we as United Methodist Christians could try to do so as well!

Holy conferencing invites others into the conversation and doesn't exclude them. Obama's speech sparked future productive conversations around dinner tables, watering holes at the office, and hallways. Likewise, holy conferencing invites people to further reflection and discussion rather than cutting off future opportunities to grow in grace and love toward others.

Holy conferencing requires spiritual maturity, self-discipline, and a desire to "move toward perfection" in love. We need to practice more, and not just for the sake of "saving the church," but for the sake of helping us fulfill our Christian commandment to love our neighbor as ourselves. Jesus says in the Gospel of John, "by this everyone will know that you are my disciples, if you have love for one another" (John 13:35).

Various Levels of Holy Conferencing

Holy conferencing provides awareness, direction, tools, and the development of skills and practices that help us talk to each other about difficult matters when there is much disagreement. Various contexts for conversation require various levels of conversation that use various practices to help us talk to each other.

The first level of holy conferencing is to "speak the truth in love" (Eph 4:15). As previously mentioned, sometimes holy conferencing is reduced to "talking nicely" with each other, or "making nice." In the state of Minnesota, it's called "Minnesota nice" and means that people are reluctant to state openly and honestly what they believe usually for fear of embarrassment or hurting others (or oneself). However, that doesn't stop them from complaining or talking badly about others who aren't present. When this happens, the person who is not present never has the opportunity to address the situation. This doesn't only happen in the state of Minnesota; there's a cultural resistance to face conflict openly and honestly and yet with love.

Holy conferencing requires that one speak one's truth to the person(s) who disagree or need to know what the conflict is. People who avoid conflict usually prefer a "shuttle diplomacy" where they speak their truth to someone else (who is in authority or in some way is a safer listener) who will then go speak their truth to others who need to know or are involved. What is lost in this "shuttle diplomacy" is the mutual search for truth that comes by speaking and listening to one another. The shuttle diplomat bears the responsibility of sharing the truth back and forth and often has the impossible task of representing the nuances as well as the actual words spoken by each group.

This happens in the church all the time. For instance, longtime members are reluctant to speak face to face. How can they possibly face each other for the next thirty years of their lives if they say the wrong words? Or because laity are afraid to address their concerns about the pastor to the pastor, they often insist on speaking to the pastor's supervisor, never having stated their concerns directly to the pastor. Likewise, Sunday school classes and study groups tend to avoid the sharing of different opinions about Scripture, faith matters, and social concerns for fear of being misunderstood and shunned from a long-established group. Yet the end result is that no one *learns* to speak the truth in love to others, sharing out of one's experience, being open to others' experiences, and even being willing to change one's heart and mind about something!

As United Methodists approached General Conference 2008, retired bishop Reuben Job reinterpreted John Wesley's historic General Rules in a book titled *Three Simple Rules*. He reminded us as United Methodists that John Wesley had three simple rules: do no harm, do good, and stay in love with God.[8] Bishop Job's way of stating the General Rules in his book puts these concepts into simple words that we all can remember.

To do no harm begins with how we speak to each other. When we refuse to speak in a way that is harmful toward another, we are holy conferencing. But consider how difficult it is to keep this simple rule!

Each of us knows of groups that are locked in conflict, sometimes over profound issues and sometimes over issues that are just plain silly. But the conflict is real, the divisions deep, and consequences often devastating. If, however, all who are involved can agree to do no harm, the *climate* in which the conflict is going on is immediately changed. How is it changed? Well, if I am to do no harm, I can no longer *gossip* about the conflict. I can no longer *speak disparagingly* about those involved in the conflict. I can no longer *manipulate the facts* of the conflict. I can no longer *diminish* those who do not agree with me and must honor each as a child of God. *I will guard my lips, my mind and my heart so that my language will not disparage, injure or wound another child of God. I must do no harm, even while I seek a common good.*[9]

The climate with which we carry on our conversations or conferencing is important. The role of the leader or the one presiding in such situations can make the climate congenial toward "speaking the truth in love" and doing no harm by setting the times, contexts, and even formats for conversations that will provide the best possible interaction between people. Gossip and disparaging conversation about others tears the community down and is often done not just one on one, but through various publications, e-mails, and other media using direct attacks or innuendos. Manipulating the facts, even when there is a disagreement about them, adds to confusion that generates more anxiety and therefore deepens the conflict. Diminishing others and making personal attacks instead of staying on the topic make it difficult for people to be in conversation with each other. Doing no harm is certainly a fundamental component of holy conferencing.

The second rule is to do good. Doing good is even more radical and endless in its possibilities for changing the dynamics we find in conflicted situations. Doing good provides a generous and gracious approach to others when we find ourselves in conflict at work, in our families, with our children or parents, and in the church. It demands staying at the table with each other. We might make a child stay at the table until the last pea is eaten, but we don't always make ourselves or encourage others to stay at the table until the last word is spoken in love. Doing good requires a strong commitment to being in community, near and far, local and global. As Job says,

I must seek what is best for those whose position and condition may be far
different from my vision for them. It will mean that I will seek to heal the
wounds of my sisters and brothers, no matter if their social position, economic condition, educational achievement, or lifestyle is radically different
from mine. It will mean that the words and acts that wound and divide
will be changed to words and acts that heal and bring together. It will mean
that movements that seek to divide and conquer will become movements
that seek to unite and empower all. It will mean that the common good
will be my first thought and what is good for me will become a secondary
thought.[10]

How can we possibly live toward such a lofty goal? Therein resides the
third rule: stay in love with God. We must practice the means of grace that
are given to us—Bible study, prayer, Holy Communion, fasting, and conferencing—in order to grow in love toward God and our neighbor. These rules
are difficult to keep but that doesn't minimize their importance and the challenge to keep them. Job believes that they may demand

> too much in the way of self-discipline . . . for many of us [it is] to agree
> with a theology and a practice too rigorous for our timid and tame com-
> mitment . . . it is not an easy rule; and it does demand a radical trust in
> God's presence, power, wisdom, and guidance and a radical obedience to
> God's leadership. Practicing our faith in the world requires our deepest
> resolve, our greatest faith, our unwavering trust, and a very, very large
> measure of God's grace.[11]

Holy conferencing is neither for the faint-hearted nor for those who
casually approach the Christian faith. We must do more than believe in our
heads or confess with our lips that Jesus Christ is Lord. We must become
practicing Christians who do no harm, do good, and stay in love with God
and therefore with our neighbor. While these rules are historically
Methodist, they are commended to all Christians!

A second level of holy conferencing is needed when there is more than a
small group and when the issues are more complex, long-standing, and
deeply divisive. At such times, the best way to be able to speak the truth in
love is to gather the diverse and invested voices, interests, and perspectives to
listen to each other and to allow the possibility of a consensus to emerge that
is healthy and healing.

Free-for-all conversations rarely bring the best out in us or in each other.
Some structure, a special format of sitting as well as talking, and guidelines

are necessary in order to provide a safe environment for people to speak and listen to each other's truth. There are many structured conversational formats.[12]

The Peacemaking Circle Process is probably one of the most widely known and used in various-sized groups. The circle process has a long tradition among indigenous people of North America and has been a gift they have given to other cultures. There are many types of settings for a Peacemaking Circle Process, including decision-making, community-building, healing, support, and the sentencing in restorative justice.

Key elements exist in all peacemaking circles. Participants gather in a circle of chairs with no table in the middle. An object of some kind is used, often called the talking piece (a direct link to the indigenous people who practiced this method), which is passed from person to person. No one can speak unless she or he is holding the talking piece. A facilitator assists the group and helps create the safe space for everyone to feel comfortable speaking his or her truth. The facilitator also makes sure that the guidelines for listening and sharing are known and kept. Decisions emerge out of consensus without everyone having to agree, although everyone must agree that they are able to live with the decision finally expressed by the group with the assistance of the facilitator.

I have used the Peacemaking Circle Process in my own experience as a pastor of a church that needed to make a difficult and emotional decision. When the emotionality of the community became rather intense and even toxic, I realized that we needed another way of talking with each other besides the free-flowing arguments that prevailed.

An organization in our community came and taught us simple methods of speaking to one another. By and large they trained us in making "I" statements and using various techniques to allow all voices—not just the loudest—to be heard. A loud, angry voice will silence others' wisdom. A loud, angry voice will encourage "group think," usually in the direction of the loud, angry voice because people are intimidated to counter it with their own truth.

A week before the important vote in the congregation, we gathered together in the basement of the church. People signed up if they wanted to speak, and each person had two minutes. In between each speaker were 10 seconds of silence, and no one was allowed to speak or make noises unless the speaker held a ceramic dove, our talking piece.

It was a powerful time. Everyone who wanted to speak spoke, and then we prayed and went home. We came back together the following week without further conversation to vote. After the announcement of the vote, it was agreed upon that no one would cheer or express disapproval. After singing and prayer, we went home to contemplate what this vote meant for our future as a faith community.

It was my first experience of using this process, and I was impressed with how hard it is for people not to interrupt and make disparaging sounds when others speak their truth. I also learned how important it is to establish the guidelines of how the process will be conducted so that everyone is empowered by them, not having to guess what will happen next and not giving anyone an advantage over another. We clearly communicated the process, although every time I've used it, some have insisted that it stifles them from fully expressing themselves. But I can't imagine how we would have made many decisions without the Peacemaking Circle Process and managed to do as little harm in reaching a final decision. This was a fundamental experience in my ministry and for that matter my faith.

Yet another level of holy conferencing is needed in larger decision-making bodies that normally use Robert's Rules of Order to discuss difficult topics. In such situations, it's important to reshape or reformat the conversation, preferably by giving the body the opportunity to approve a process through its regular means of decision-making (such as Robert's Rules of Order). The reshaping or reformatting I've used is largely an adaptation of the Peacemaking Circle Process.

At the 2006 Annual Conference in Minnesota, we reshaped or reformatted our way of making decisions about nine controversial petitions on homosexuality. We established the guidelines, empowering the body to agree to them by voting on them. A few amendments to the process were presented as legislation, but as a result, the commitment to the process was deepened. Once again, some people resisted the idea that they would not have the opportunity to speak whenever or however they wished.

Our process included suspension of Robert's Rules of Order for an established period of time. During that time, delegates were given the opportunity to go to the microphone and speak their truth on the topic in general or on the petitions without the hindrance of parliamentary procedure. In most cases people wanted to speak from their hearts rather than bending around a parliamentary procedure like the making of an amendment in order to make a speech. The microphones were arranged in such a way that, as the one presiding, I could call on one microphone after another in a circular fashion, and we were able to alternately hear voices in favor of the petitions and those against them.

For 1.5 hours as we had agreed, anyone could come to a mic and speak her or his heart about homosexuality and/or the specific petitions for ninety seconds. Ninety seconds doesn't sound like a long time, but not all used their full time and few went beyond it. As a result, people felt empowered, listened to, and less "beat up" by each other, as such difficult conversations can make people feel.

When the time was over, we prayed, and the next day we voted by ballot with only the opportunity for amendments allowed. No amendments were made and the delegates voted. When the ballots returned, I asked them not to express themselves verbally in favor or disapproval as I read them. We prayed and they quietly left the room for lunch. While some people didn't like the outcome of the petitions, most of those who were part of the process felt it made a painful discussion less painful and strengthened community in the midst of diversity.

Since then, holy conferencing has affected the way in which we receive petitions and motions and the way we handle ballots and voting. We employ parts of the process—or the complete process—when discussing difficult issues, and not only sexuality issues. Perhaps most importantly, when we stop and remind ourselves to be in holy conferencing, we are reminding ourselves that we're called to be set apart in our speech, actions, and relationships as Christians.

At the United Methodist General Conference in 2008, there was no established format for reshaping its way of conferencing. At no time was Robert's Rules of Order suspended, nor was there a plan given to discuss a matter differently; this level of holy conferencing was never used. As a result, holy conferencing stayed on the level of "speaking the truth in love" while trying to do as little harm to each other as possible and even at times trying to do good through these difficult conversations. In a body of about 1,000 people from all over the world, holy conferencing had an impact on the spirit of the conference as mentioned earlier, but many hope that it will be taken further by reshaping the plenary discussions on sensitive matters in the future.

In addition, holy conferencing will continue between General Conferences (which occur every four years) by finding ways to keep us speaking our truth in love, staying at the table in spite of our differences, and growing in our relationships with God and one another. If we practice in between times, we may be better practitioners and ultimately learn new peacemaking skills for all aspects of our lives, not just church.

On August 1, 2007, the I-35W Bridge across the Mississippi River in Minneapolis collapsed within thirteen seconds, killing thirteen persons and injuring more than one hundred. Those of us who live in Minnesota have become amateur bridge engineers since the collapse, trying to learn what caused it to happen. For whatever reasons, the gussets gave way, but the most tragic result was that the bridge didn't have a redundancy system. Without a redundancy system in the design, once the gussets gave way and the bridge began to collapse, nothing was in place to stop the disaster for even a short time. If it had a redundancy system, once the gussets gave way the collapse would have been halted or slowed down so that people could have gotten out of harm's way.

The United Methodist Church, like most denominations, has lots of structure as indicated by our conferences—charge/church conferences, annual conferences, jurisdictional conferences, and a General Conference. We say that we are a "connectional" church because of these conferences that bring us together for worship, fellowship, and decision-making.

Yet, like a bridge, we can collapse if we don't have a redundancy system in our connection. Relationships are our redundancy system in all our organizations and communities, including the church. In all our relationships, we need to learn practices that help us do no harm, do good, and stay in love with God and our neighbor. Through holy conferencing and the practices it gives us, we can learn to stay at the table with each other when we want to push back and away from each other. Holy conferencing is a design to remind us that as we mutually search for truth in complex and diverse community, we can strengthen our own faith (as a means of grace) and our relationships with each other.

My hope is that as United Methodist Christians, we will grow in our awareness and practice of holy conferencing wherever we are and with whomever we are in disagreement so that we can "move on toward perfection [in love]" as John Wesley encouraged us to do. There certainly are lots of opportunities to practice holy conferencing!

Notes

1. Stephen L. Carter, *Civility: Manners, Morals, and the Etiquette of Democracy* (New York: Harper Perennial) 11–12.

2. "Minutes of Several Conversations between the Rev. Mr. Wesley and Others," in *Addresses, Essays, Letters*, vol. 8 of *The Works of John Wesley*, ed. Thomas Jackson (3rd ed.; London, 1831 [CD-ROM]; Franklin TN: Providence, 1995) question 48.

3. Parker Palmer, Earl Lectures, Berkeley CA, 28 January 1992.

4. John Wesley, *Preface to Sermons on Several Occasions*, §§ 9–10, in *Sermons I*, ed. Albert C. Outler, vol. 1 of the Bicentennial Edition of the Works of John Wesley (Nashville: Abingdon Press, 1976–) 107.

5. *The Book of Discipline* historically states the governance of the Methodist Church since its U.S. origins in 1784. It undergoes change every four years at the General Conference.

6. *The Doctrines and Discipline of the Methodist Episcopal Church* (New York: Eaton & Mains, 1904) 127–28.

7. Barack Obama, "A More Perfect Union," speech delivered at Constitution Center, Philadelphia PA, 18 March 2008. Transcript available: http://www.cnn.com/2008/POLITICS/03/18/obama.transcript/index.html.

8. John Wesley's original language for the General Rules was "do no harm, do good, and attend upon all the ordinances of God."

9. Reuben P. Job, *Three Simple Rules: A Wesleyan Way of Living* (Nashville: Abingdon Press, 2007) 22.

10. Ibid., 42–43.

11. Ibid., 24.

12. See Ron Kraybill & Evelyn Wright, *The Little Book of Cool Tools for Hot Topics: Group Tools to Facilitate Meetings When Things Are Hot* (Intercourse PA: Good Books, 2006) for various ways to facilitate holy conferencing in local settings.

Chapter 6

The Minister as Friend: Civility in Practice

Thomas R. McKibbens,
Pastor of First Baptist Church, Worcester, Massachusetts

Ministers tend to build their own concept of ministry by trying different approaches that they have seen others do. How do they go about the tasks of ministry without exploring the ways others have done it? With every sermon they preach, unseen people stand with them who have inspired them. Those unseen visitors preach along with the minister; it is inevitable. How do ministers relate to church members, to the community, to colleagues, and to larger national and world issues? How do they go about hospital visitation, personal counseling, crisis intervention, and personality conflicts? How do they approach meetings with committees and staff? How and to what degree does a minister engage in budget preparation and building supervision?

Thankfully, such questions do not require the reinvention of the wheel. Much of the professional education of ministers is an examination of the ways others have approached those essential tasks, with the expectation that the minister will draw out the best from those examples and formulate ways of ministry that work best for the minister's own personality and situation in life. In all of these pursuits, the minister must model Christian civility.

Examples for ministry are important for the growth of any minister's unique style. Every budding minister needs to experiment with different models, especially in the early years of ministry. In my experiences of teaching in several theological schools, I have seen a number of models apparent in student sermons. In the early years of my teaching, I could pick out little "Billy Grahams" who mimicked his style and mannerisms, even his North Carolina accent. Later, as more television preachers became prominent, I could detect other well-known ministers in the ways budding preachers carried themselves and spoke with certain styles. At Harvard, I detected some little "Peter Gomeses" with a slightly British accent!

Theological schools themselves seem to develop a certain style of ministry, often following the lead of some respected professor. I was once asked if the church I served could provide a "neutral pulpit" for a minister to preach before a pastor search committee. After the sermon, one of my members informed me that what we had just heard was "the Chicago style of preaching." I was left alone to figure out what that meant! It is not uncommon, however, for laity to guess correctly what seminary a minister attended merely by listening to the style of preaching.

Ministry as Therapy

Clinical pastoral education, a common component in nearly all American seminaries, began in the 1920s under the leadership of Anton Boisen and Richard Cabot. Boisen was chaplain at Worcester State Hospital. In the summer of 1924 he began with four theological students for a summer of intensive study and work with the patients in Worcester, Massachusetts. In successive summers the number of students quickly multiplied until by the end of the decade they numbered twenty-nine.

Richard C. Cabot, a member of a distinguished New England family, was a physician at Boston's Massachusetts General Hospital and a professor of Clinical Medicine at Harvard Medical School. After introducing clinical training for social workers at Massachusetts General Hospital in 1905, he turned his attention to the preparation of pastors and helped found the Council for the Clinical Training of Theological Students in January 1930, serving as its president until 1935. In his later years he became a professor of Sociology and Applied Christianity at Andover Newton Theological School.

The essential element of clinical training for theological students was that they be introduced under trained guidance to what Boisen called "living human documents," so that they could grapple with real human issues of life and death. This intense immersion into actual real-life problems brought the theory from the classrooms of the seminaries "to the bedside, to the bereaved, to the dying, to the invalid, to the aged and to the delinquent," as Cabot described it in 1935.[1] While theological students gain great insight into the problems of others, clinical training also has provided an important element of self-insight for the students. Many ministers look back at clinical training as one of the most profound and life-changing experiences in their theological formation.

The rapid rise of clinical pastoral education can be understood in the larger context of world events. Two world wars brought home many soldiers with what was earlier known as "shell shock" and later called post-traumatic stress disorder. Pastors felt totally inadequate to deal with the serious problems of church members who had experienced trauma and witnessed atrocities on or off the battlefield. Paul Tillich observed that churches began to realize something was wrong in the training of ministers when troubled Christians began to turn first to psychoanalysis rather than to their pastors for help.[2]

Families had to deal with intense problems of a soldier's reentry into peacetime life. This was certainly not the first time soldiers had come home from wars with problems, but clinical pastoral education gave the clergy a level of training that had never before been experienced. Ministers in earlier generations were, in the words of Alexander Maclaren, "pitch-forked into prominent positions at once," where they would struggle with critical human situations in obscurity and with little help other than their own wits and common sense.[3]

A second impetus for the clinical training of pastors was the Social Gospel Movement of the early years of the twentieth century. As historian Allison Stokes points out, the most concrete products of the Social Gospel Movement were the institutional church and the religious social settlement.[4] The institutional church, with all its varied organizations and committees, demanded from the pastor a level of administration not known before. Endless committee meetings and the constant supervision of staff in many cases took priority over pastoral care. Critical human needs calling for pastoral attention were left unmet. People needed to turn to someone who was skilled in listening and able to help them with their problems. When their pastor was too busy in the administration of an institutional church, they began to turn to other helping professions, specifically to psychiatrists who were incorporating the insights of psychoanalysis.

The popularity of psychoanalysis, then, is a third major factor in the rise of the therapeutic model for ministry. The towering figure of Sigmund Freud had a profound effect on the profession of psychiatry in the 1920s. Anton Boisen was deeply indebted to Freud for insights that informed his life and thought, but he never substituted Freudianism for Christianity. For him, psychoanalytical theory was always a tool to help in understanding human personality, never an end in itself. In fact, as Stokes makes clear, Boisen was fearful of the misuse of Freudian psychoanalytical theory in clinical pastoral education.

Within the psychoanalytic movement, there have developed a number of schools of thought that often compete with one another. Clinical pastoral education traditions in various parts of the country sometimes insist that they are not Freudian, but Jungian, for example. Nevertheless, they are all deeply indebted to psychoanalytic theory, which began with Freud, just as all contemporary schools of theology, whether or not they call themselves Barthian, are still indebted to Karl Barth.

A further and often overlooked factor in the rise of clinical pastoral education has been the Progressive Education Movement growing out of the work of John Dewey and others. Steering away from a style of teaching that emphasized rote memorization and drill, the progressives aimed to lead students to observe, to reason, and to relate critically to their world as well as to learn certain facts. Teachers in the progressive movement were not all-knowing masters whose task was to pour information into the minds of students. Rather, the teacher became a guide, a fellow discoverer of truth, and even a friend. While later interpreters of Dewey sometimes distorted his theory into methods synonymous with permissiveness and unbridled license, Dewey himself emphasized both solid content as well as active student participation in the process of learning.

Dewey believed that education had to be integrated with real-life situations, not preparation for a remote future. In what he called "My Pedagogic Creed," published in 1897 while he and his wife were running a successful laboratory school at the University of Chicago, he stated his conviction "that the only true education comes through the stimulation of the child's powers by the demands of the social situations in which he finds himself."[5] It is not difficult to see the influence of the progressive movement on the clinical pastoral education movement. Using the basic pedagogical principles of John Dewey, clinical education for pastors took students out of the classroom and stimulated their powers, to use Dewey's phrase, by the demands of critical human situations.

Ministry as therapy has been immensely helpful to many ministers and churches. My description of another approach is not to reject the tremendous benefits of the therapeutic model, but to redirect it. For unfortunately, clinical pastoral education has sometimes become so enamored with the aura of psychiatry, so caught up in the use of psychological language, and so convinced that the psychoanalytic approach to counseling is and should be the centerpiece of ministry, that it has sometimes relegated the distinctiveness of the Christian gospel to an incidental sidelight of ministry. There are those, such as Philip Rieff, who applaud what he calls the "triumph of the thera-peutic."[6] He assumes that people are no longer religious, and therefore church leaders should become avowedly therapists, administering a thera-peutic institution under the justifying mandate that Jesus himself was primarily a therapist.

Social historian Christopher Lasch, on the other hand, has been an out-spoken critic of this vision of a society run by what he calls "a psychiatric priesthood."[7] He challenges the practitioners of psychiatry for rejecting Freud's modest goals and becoming a new religion, promising the traditional consolations of personal mastery, spiritual peace, and meaning. O. Hobart Mowrer pointed out that the danger for a young minister is in the attempt to solve every problem of faith through psychological analysis. This is compli-cated by the fact that throughout clinical pastoral education, careful training has been given in knowing when to refer a person to a psychiatrist.

In the minister's own eyes, clergy are often perceived as second- or third-tier practitioners in crisis response. Mowrer calls for a return to the practice of confession: "We have tried to ignore and by-pass the very notion of guilt and sin; but it won't work," he claims. "The gospel of sin and salvation . . . is not one of bondage but of liberation, hope, and strength; and we must, I believe, return to it in all seriousness."[8] Perhaps it should not be surprising to clergy that the well-known work by Karl Menninger, *Whatever Became of Sin?* came not from a fundamentalist preacher, but from the psychiatric com-munity itself![9]

Theologian Hans Küng offers a helpful distinction between the terms "emancipation" and "redemption." Emancipation, says Küng, is a human action, something done by humanity for humanity. Redemption, on the other hand, has a transcendent element. "Redemption means liberation . . . by God, not any self-redemption. . . ."[10] Following Küng's theological lead, we can say that redemption cannot be replaced by psychological emancipa-tion through psychoanalysis. It is the age-old mistake of assuming that human suffering can be abolished by humanity's own power, by the applica-tion of psychoanalysis. Christian faith claims that redemption brings a level of freedom to a depth that emancipation cannot reach.

I have spent a considerable amount of time discussing ministry as ther-apy because that is a popular approach to ministry in today's religious culture and, in my judgment, it has most influenced church communities. After three quarters of a century, the therapeutic model is beginning to show some of its drawbacks in spite of all the good it has produced. We see ministers who have ditched all theological language for psychobabble or pop psychology.

We see ministers who are well trained in recognizing neuroses and psychoses, but have little grasp of the deeper theological notions of sin and redemption. We see ministers who are perfectly capable of sustaining long-term counseling relationships with individuals, but clearly at a loss when working with small groups in the church. We see ministers who are good listeners to parishioners in counseling, but are hesitant to offer prayer for or with them. The value of therapeutic training encompassed in clinical pastoral education is not questioned here; rather, I am raising the issue of whether ministry as therapy should be the singular approach for ministers in the twenty-first century.

The Minister as Chief Executive Officer

Another contemporary approach that competes in some quarters with ministry as therapy is the Chief Executive Officer (CEO) approach. The minister as CEO places great weight on the biblical text found in Hebrews 13:17 ("Obey your leaders and submit to them, for they are keeping watch over your souls and will give an account"). The Episcopal polity practiced by the Roman Catholic Church as well as the Anglican wing of Christianity has always possessed an element of this approach, while denominations with Congregationalist polities such as the UCC, the Baptists, and those from other free church traditions have somehow managed to function with what some have called a "mobocracy."

The CEO approach is a revised and contemporary version of the third-century plea of Cyprian to "do nothing without the bishop!" The bishop, in other words, was the ruler of the church. The fourth-century Syrian church manual titled *The Apostolic Constitutions* insisted on obedience to the bishop by the laity. The one who hears the bishop hears Christ, and the one who rejects the bishop rejects Christ and thus God the Father (2.20). This manual outdoes even Cyprian in lauding the authority of the clergy:

> The bishop is the minister of the word, the guardian of knowledge, the mediator between God and you when he worships with you. He is the teacher of piety. He is your father after God, having begotten you for adoption by water and the Spirit. He is your ruler and governor; he is your king and potentate; he is your earthly "god after God," who ought to be honored by you. (2.26)[11]

Such expressions of what we could call the early CEO model can be traced through the Middle Ages to the Renaissance and the Reformation to the modern age, but not in every part of the church. There were always those, like Origen in the East and Augustine in the West, who had serious reservations about such an authoritarian ministry. What is clear in any era is that pastoral authority often increases when the church feels under attack and is thus insecure. In the time of Cyprian, the Christians at Carthage had been confronted with a fierce persecution under Emperor Decius (AD 249–251), and there was schism in the church as a consequence of debate over the readmission of those who had lapsed during the persecution. The solution, in Cyprian's view, was to reaffirm the power of the CEO—the bishop.

The contemporary argument is similar. The conservative evangelical wing of Christianity, particularly the fundamentalists, believes that the church is under attack by what is often called "the religion of secular humanism." Their explanation for rising crime rates and other ills of society frequently rests on hot-button issues like the Supreme Court's decision to disallow prescribed prayer in public schools, the legalization of abortion, sex education curricula in the schools (particularly regarding homosexuality), and violence in the media.

That is their perceived attack from without. But there is also a perceived attack from within, which is focused on what in their view is a watering down of true doctrine by liberalism taught in seminaries and seeping into the churches. Thus they emphasize the plenary verbal inspiration of the Scriptures and mount attacks on the use of critical methodology in the study of the Bible. Supporters of the CEO approach to ministry have reestablished an emphasis on the pastor as the locus of authority in the church. In 1988, the massive Southern Baptist Convention met in San Antonio, Texas, and passed a resolution that undermined their historic Baptist emphasis on the priesthood of the believer. In part, the resolution read,

WHEREAS, The doctrine of the Priesthood of the Believer can be used to justify the undermining of pastoral authority in the local church . . .
Be it further RESOLVED, That we affirm that this doctrine in no way gives license to misinterpret, explain away, demythologize, or extrapolate out elements of the supernatural in the Bible; and
Be it further RESOLVED, that the doctrine of the Priesthood of the Believer in no way contradicts the biblical understanding of the role, responsibility, and authority of the pastor which is seen in the command to the local church in Hebrews 13:17. . . .

In their view, the only way to safeguard the purity of the church is for the pastor to be a ruler over the church. This same understanding is clearly seen in the Promise Keepers movement, which advocates the same authoritarian rule of the husband over the family, even if it is benevolent. Their sense that the church is besieged is matched by their sense that the family is besieged, and the solution is to reestablish a clear line of authority with the husband at the top of the family and the pastor at the top of the church. In a sermon in a Texas church, Professor Bruce Ware of the Southern Baptist Theological Seminary even blamed spousal abuse on the wives who refuse to submit to their husbands! Both husband and pastor are in the place of the CEO. It is a clearly a male-dominated business model.

The Minister as Friend

This brings us to another approach to ministry: the minister as friend. Apparently, there was a long-standing tradition within the early church that Abraham was called "the friend of God." In reality, there is no particular place in the early stories of Abraham that designates him God's friend, but only later traditions, such as the Isaiah 41 passage in which the voice of God refers to "Abraham, my friend." Scholars even debate over that translation, and the Hebrew word may not be "friend" but something like "beloved." But all scholarly debate aside, the fact remains that there was a strong tradition that Abraham was called "the friend of God."

One other tradition should be mentioned here: in the descriptions of Moses meeting with God, there is a fascinating phrase found in Exodus 33:11: "Thus the LORD used to speak to Moses face to face, as one speaks to a friend." So we have two great patriarchs whom later generations remembered as having a special friendship with God.

To conceive of God as Friend engenders immediate resistance from those who fear too casual a relationship with God, as though God is a divine chum, a kind of loyal sidekick in the journey of life. An appropriate distance and awe are required for our conception of God. After all, the model prayer taught by Jesus did not begin, "Our Buddy, who art in heaven."

On the other hand, an argument can be made that friendship need not imply equality. The tradition of Abraham as a friend of God certainly did not imply that Abraham was equal to God. In the familiar New Testament passage found in James 2:23, for example, it says that "Abraham believed God, and it was reckoned to him as righteousness," and he was called the friend of God. The writer of that epistle makes a clear connection between Abraham's believing God as the basis of Abraham's friendship with God. He never implies that God and Abraham were somehow equals, or that this was a kind of committee of two deciding on the move from Haran. God is always God the Creator; Abraham is always human.

What I am moving toward here is the thought that friendship with God need not imply a chummy relationship. God is always God. But is it not possible to have a deep friendship with someone who is not our equal? The conception of God as Divine Friend is far more personal than philosophical terms such as "Unmoved Mover" or "Ground of All Being" or even "President of the Universe." Those terms may work in an objective, philosophical way of thinking, but they leave many people cold. At the same time, the conception of God as Divine Friend is gender neutral, which is not a light issue in our day.

John Bunyan seems to have this conception of the divine in a passage from *Pilgrim's Progress*, in which Christian comes within sight of the heavenly city, set high on a hill. Between him and the heavenly city is a deep river with no bridge. He must cross that river in order to reach the heavenly city. When Christian begins to cross the river in great fear, he feels the presence of a friend named Hopeful by his side. When Christian begins to sink in the water, he cries out to his friend Hopeful, "I sink in deep waters, and billows go over my head . . . !" Then Hopeful says to Christian, "Be of good cheer, my brother. I feel the bottom, and it is good."[12]

This image of the Divine Friend who will be by our side, even in the deepest of waters, carries a profound meaning as the basis for our fundamental relationship with God. I am proposing that we revisit this image on an experiential level in the lives of our churches and as an understanding of the lifelong role of the minister.

Friends in Need

On another level, there is a surprising amount of contemporary interest in the subject of friendship, particularly among feminist thinkers, who have produced over the past few decades a body of literature on the study of the significance of friendship in our society both for men and women, highlighting basic differences between the nature of male and female friendships. Some scholars and service practitioners have concluded that male friendships are not as nurturing or as intimate as female friendships, but regardless of that ongoing debate, they all agree that male friendship has been held up as the historic ideal. The significance of female friendship has been all but ignored and often ridiculed.

Letty Cottin Pogrebin, in her book titled *Among Friends,* points out that "Hundreds if not thousands of writers and social scientists from Homer to Freud have shared the view that women are incapable of deep, enduring friendship." She quotes Montaigne, who claimed in his sixteenth-century essay "On Friendship" that "the ordinary capacity of women is inadequate for the communion and fellowship which is the muse of the sacred bond of friendship, nor does their soul feel firm enough to endure the strain of so tight and durable a knot."[13]

With that kind of nonsense in our philosophical background, current research, particularly feminist research, has attempted to demonstrate just the opposite. Men may be the ones who have trouble with deep friendship. On the other hand, women writers are frequently the ones talking about the importance of deep friendships. According to Pogrebin, if there were a college course on friendship, men would get an "incomplete" and women would not only earn an "A" but also tutor their classmates! That may hit some of us as hyperbole, but this is the tone of much of the contemporary writing on friendship.

The intergenerational and intra-family model of Naomi and Ruth is an interesting study for women. Naomi is Ruth's mother-in-law. Throw out all the old mother-in-law stories here; this is genuine devoted friendship. Ruth was a Moabite, one of a people hated by the Jews for centuries. That is precisely the reason that when Ruth married Naomi's son, they had to leave Bethlehem and go to the land of the Moabites. Theirs was an interracial marriage. When Ruth's husband died, and Ruth said to Naomi,

> Do not press me to leave you
> or to turn back from following you!
> Where you go, I will go;
> Where you lodge, I will lodge;
> Your people shall be my people,
> and your God my God.
> Where you die, I will die—
> there will I be buried.
> May the Lord do thus and so to me,
> and more as well,
> if even death parts me from you! (Ruth 1:16)

Essentially, Ruth was saying, "I am not returning to my own race of people. I am devoted to your friendship and I want to go back to Bethlehem with you." It is a powerful story.

Ruth and Naomi were two women of different generations and different racial backgrounds in a deep and lifelong friendship. Like many of the women in the current research on friendship, these women shared their deepest feelings with one another. Naomi coached Ruth on how to be successful in a romantic relationship with Boaz. Naomi even went so far as to tell Ruth what soap to use and what perfume to wear, as if their lives depended on it!

Regardless of the apparent differences in male and female friendship, to say nothing of the difficult thicket of male-female friendships in our culture, contemporary research agrees on the crucial need for deep friendship in a depersonalized and mobile society. Apart from scholarship on the subject of friendship, ministers observe and experience the value of deep friendship on a daily basis.

Friends in Conflict

If we conceive of the church as a communion of friends, then how do we account for church conflict? Diane Kessler's book titled *God's Simple Gift: Meditations on Friendship and Spirituality* includes powerful insights on friendship. In one of her meditations she discusses what she calls "word wars" among friends, and out of her own reading of the New Testament she catalogues the surprising number of conflicts among friends.[14] Jesus and Peter, for example, had a severe conflict over the decision to travel to Jerusalem. The disciples themselves argued as they traveled, "Who is the greatest among us?" Then look at the conflict Jesus had in his own family, who perhaps had hoped that he, the eldest, would carry on the family business, but instead he broke the tradition and traipsed off with a group of friends on a kind of itinerant preaching mission. The Gospel of Mark uses the word "restrain" in describing what Jesus' family wanted to do with him—"restrain," as if he were out of his mind (Mark 3:21)! The epistles are rife with examples of church conflict, as when Paul writes to the church at Corinth, "It has been reported to me that there are quarrels among you" (1 Cor 1:11). That has to be one of the great understatements in the Bible!

The conclusion is that the church has a long way to go in dealing creatively with friendship. Many churches experience conflict that would make the Corinthians nod in recognition. Often ministers return from large denominational gatherings bewildered over the animosity and wrangling that approaches loathing between sides on certain difficult debates. Among the contemporary writers on friendship is Mary Hunt, whose book title sums up the matter: *Fierce Tenderness.*[15] Those two apparently opposite words, she believes, should be coupled when it comes to friendship, for it takes both fierceness and tenderness to make a true friendship. Tenderness plays itself out in compassion, and fierceness plays itself out in justice.

However we play it in the church, it could be that the church is one of the best hopes we have, for the church and its sister institutions provide a context in which there is a mandate to be friends. The church is called to tender love and fierce justice. We have largely left the image of friendship to the Quakers, who call themselves the Society of Friends, but perhaps they have been on target all along. When the early church remembered Jesus as saying to his disciples, "I do not call you servant any longer, because the servant does not know what the master is doing; but I have called you friends . . ." (John 15:15), it sounds like a promotion. Servant is not enough; friendship is a higher calling, a fierce and tender friendship. Of all the approaches to ministry, ministry as friendship may be most suited for our contentious age. It certainly provides ample opportunities for practicing Christian civility.

Friends in Practice

The difficulty, of course, is in practice. How do ministers model a ministry of friendship? How do they walk the tightrope of relating to church members as friends without being too close to some and being accused of favoritism? How do they relate to each other in the larger context of associations and denominations in which there is sometimes fierce competition among ministers for position and power? Any model of ministry must pose these practical and pertinent questions.

The beginning of an answer, of course, must start with self-friendship. If the minister is not a self-friend, has not come to terms with herself, has not made peace inside his own skin, then it is difficult for his or her friendship to be authentic with others. It is worth asking how Jesus could have been friends with such a diverse group of disciples. They ranged from fishermen to a tax collector to a zealot, to say nothing of the many unnamed men and women who followed him and were part of his extended family of disciples. The diversity among the twelve is a miniature of the diversity within churches and denominations. Yet Jesus himself was at peace. His own self-worth gave him the security to be friends with others who were quite diverse in their beliefs. There was no great need on the part of Jesus to confine himself to friendships with those who were like him.

A revealing text about his friendship in the Gospel of Mark pictures Jesus as aware that one of the disciples would betray him. Who knows how he knew? There is no indication in the text itself that his knowledge of the betrayal was in any way supernatural; it could have been that word reached him from another source that Judas had betrayed him. Yet at the final meal with his disciples, Judas was seated with the rest, and Jesus made his announcement that one of them would betray him.

It is stunning in the text that all of them, every last one of them, "began to be distressed and to say to him one after another, 'Surely, not I?'" That is to say, every one of them knew deep down that there was the potential for betrayal in his heart. No wonder they were distressed! No wonder they had self-doubts! Surely they must have thought, *Did I say something? Did I do something? Did I, in an unguarded moment, make a mistake that would bring harm to Jesus?* These are questions any of us can ask at any time about our friendships with others.

The other striking thing about this text is Jesus' statement that the one who would betray him is "one who is eating with me . . . one who is dipping bread into the bowl with me." What is it about enjoying meals that bonds people together? What is the strange alchemy of food and friendship? Perhaps it is the unspoken recognition that in the act of eating together, all pretenses vanish. Every last one of us, faithful and unfaithful, brave and fearful, loyal and disloyal, has a need for nourishment. Food is the leveler of royalty and commoner. Getting our knees under a table together changes the equation. No longer are we in an over-under relationship. No longer is one dominating another. There is an unspoken equality found in eating together.

Long ago Christians made the decision that at the center of worship would be a cross and a table. The cross represents a love that will stop at nothing, not even death, to reach the beloved. It represents the extent to which love will go to maintain that fierce and tender love. The table, on the other hand, is a common ground for every person who yearns to experience that fierce and tender love. Friendship is nourished around a table. Many such tables in many a church have the phrase, "This do in remembrance of me," carved on the front for all to see. One hopes the church will remember that Jesus was willing to eat with his betrayer.

When he announced his willingness to do that, each disciple wondered if he were the betrayer! Such is life in ministry—loyalty and betrayal around a common table, loyalty and betrayal even within the same person! Jesus practiced this approach to ministry, and it is the approach I commend for ministry in today's war-torn and economically and socially stratified world.

Ministry as friendship extends beyond friendship within the church or denomination or even religion. Friends, as countless examples have demonstrated over the centuries, are not confined to the same belief system, the same race, the same economic status, the same neighborhood. How we define "neighbor" in our culture may be one of the crucial questions any individual or church or nation can pose. Can we be friends with others based not on a belief system, but on a common humanity? Can the idea of agape, that marvelous New Testament word that draws us all toward working for the common good of all people, drive the church toward a new level of friendship?

In my current ministry as pastor of a relatively large church in a New England city, I saw that one of our community's great needs was for churches of all sizes to come together for a common goal. In our city are hundreds of immigrants from other countries who often subsist on low income. Food pantries and meal programs were strained to the limit. There was genuine hunger in our community.

I also saw that many of the churches reaching out most effectively to low-income residents of the city were tiny storefront churches. Those churches often had no contact with the larger, more established churches in the community, the ones we often call "tall-steeple churches." So I gathered a few friends to discuss the problem, and we decided to call together the pastors of as many of the community churches as possible. We knew that the storefront churches often looked with some hesitancy toward the established churches in the community, so we built the meeting around a meal. Come for lunch, we said, for we want to know you. We can learn from you. And the truth is that we could and did learn from them. One of the pastors of a storefront church wrote me a thank-you note that expressed her appreciation for being invited. She had never been in one of the large churches.

The result of that meeting was a series of meetings that eventually formed a new organization built around the needs of hunger in the community. New relationships were built that transcended theology and cultural traditions. New ties between the churches and the community were forged, eventually bringing in the local government, local news media, food pantries, and meal programs. Churches were energized and new programs were established, but most importantly, friendships were forged between pastors and laypeople who had never known one another before. The ministry of hospitality served as a springboard for a larger ministry of hunger relief, which continues to this day as a platform for other ministries based on the friendship among pastors forged by that one act of hospitality.

The next time someone says, "Let's do lunch," hear it as more than a meeting to do business. Hear it as a way of ministry, an invitation to meet on the level ground of humanity, and a proposal for a way of listening and speaking that follows the example of Jesus and opens a pathway to hope in the church and the world.

Notes

1. Richard Cabot, "Clinical Training on the Earhart Foundation," *The Institution Bulletin: Andover Newton Theological School* (October 1935): 4–5.

2. Paul Tillich, "The Impact of Pastoral Psychology on Theological Thought," in *The Ministry and Mental Health,* ed. Hans Hofmann (New York: Association Press, 1960) 15–16.

3. Quoted in David Williamson, *The Life of Alexander Maclaren* (London: James Clarke and Co., n.d.) 200.

4. Allison Stokes, *Ministry After Freud* (New York: Pilgrim Press, 1985) 14.

5. John Dewey, "My Pedagogic Creed," *The School Journal,* 1897, quoted in Samuel J. Braun and Esther P. Edwards, *History and Theory of Early Childhood Education* (Worthington OH: Charles A. Jones Publishing Company) 101.

6. Philip Rieff, *The Triumph of the Therapeutic: Uses of Faith After Freud* (Harper & Row, 1966).

7. Christopher Lasch, *The Culture of Narcissism, American Life in an Age of Diminishing Expectations* (New York: W.W. Norton, 1979).

8. O. Hobart Mowrer, *The Crisis in Psychiatry and Religion* (Princeton: D. Van Nostrand Co., Inc., 1961) 78.

9. Karl Menninger, *Whatever Became of Sin?* (New York: Hawthorn Books, Inc., 1974).

10. Hans Küng, *On Being a Christian,* trans. Edward Quinn (New York: Doubleday & Co., 1968) 430.

11. *Apostolic Constitutions* 2:26. See Alexander Roberts and James Donaldson, ed., *The Ante-Nicene Fathers,* vol. 7 (Grand Rapids: Wm. B. Eerdmans Publishing Company, 1951) 410.

12. John Bunyan, *The Pilgrim's Progress* (New York: The New American Library, Inc., 1964) 143.

13. Letty Cottin Pogrebin, *Among Friends* (New York: McGraw-Hill, 1987) 252.

14. Diane Kessler, *God's Simple Gift: Meditations on Friendship and Spirituality* (Valley Forge: Judson Press, 1988).

15. Mary Hunt, *Fierce Tenderness* (New York: HarperCollins, 1989).

Chapter 7

Christian Civility on the Internet

Wade Burleson,
Pastor of Emmanuel Baptist Church, Enid, Oklahoma

"The ultimate aim of civility and good manners is to please: to please one's guest or to please one's host," writes popular food critic and etiquette guru Claudia Roden.[1] Yet there are times when differences cause an air of disagreeableness among friends. During those times of difficulty, we may not always achieve civility's *aim*, but we can continue to display civility's *attributes* faithfully. By descriptive definition, the Christian life is one of principle, as we Christians live out Christ's commands on earth. The greatest of these commands is "to love God and one another,"[2] but sometimes we discover attempts to fulfill this command, particularly love to God, will cause other people displeasure. It is during these occasions of conflict that the aim of civility (i.e., "pleasing others") must become subordinate to the dictates of our own consciences. George Washington memorized 110 rules of civility as a boy, with the last rule being, "Labor to keep alive in thy breast that little spark of Celestial fire called Conscience, for Conscience to an evil man is a never dying worm, but unto a good man it's a perpetual feast."[3] When the times comes that we sit at a feast prepared by conscience, it should be consumed while sitting at the table of civility.

In December 2005 I began an Internet blog to express my conscientious objection to two new doctrinal policies approved by the trustees of the International Mission Board.[4] After consistently voicing opposition for the proposed policies in the months prior to the vote to adopt them, once the doctrinal policies were approved and became official board policy in November 2005, I went public with my objections by placing my arguments against the policies on the Internet. I miserably failed in fulfilling the *aim* of civility (being pleasing), since the trustees who pushed for the policies read my public writings, became quite *displeased*, and recommended to the SBC

that I be removed as a trustee of the International Mission Board. Such a recommendation had never been attempted by a Southern Baptist trustee board
in the previous 165-year history of our Convention.[5] The IMB trustees
unanimously reversed their recommendation for my removal eight weeks
after making it,[6] but the extraordinary measure IMB trustee leaders took to
remove one of their own shows the power the Internet possesses to cause
conflict among Christians.

Communicating by *writing on the Internet* is different from every other
form of communication. It differs from the written word contained in published books because the Internet offers instantaneous production of what is
written. It varies from phone conversations in that there is an inability to
hear the tone of the content's author. It is different from television production in that the reader cannot see the writer's facial expressions or body
mannerisms to help understand his or her intent. It differs from all the forms
of communication mentioned above in that the entire world has immediate
access to what one writes. The sheer power of the Internet is in the speed and
wide distribution of what is written and published on it. "It is no exaggera-
tion to conclude that the Internet has achieved, and continues to achieve, the
most participatory marketplace of mass speech that this country—and
indeed the world—has yet seen," wrote the erudite George Will nearly a
dozen years ago.[7]

International Mission Board trustee leaders reacted to my Internet blog
precisely because of the inherent power of the Internet. My arguments
against the new doctrinal policies were not unfamiliar (trustees had heard
them all before), but rather, the Internet distributed my words to a far wider
and more disproportionate audience than those who had access to the reasoning of the trustees who sought passage of the policies. The issue was never
about broken confidentiality. Having served as chairman of multiple boards,
president of the Oklahoma Baptist General Convention for two terms, and
parliamentarian for our state convention for years, I understand corporate
ethics and have always been careful to follow Terrence Crawford's highly
respected *10 Commandments for Board Members*, including the seventh commandment of confidentiality.[8] I wrote on my blog what I thought, reasoned,
and had already said countless times to my fellow trustees. But the moment
I started the blog, something dramatic changed. Simply understood, I had
tapped into a powerful medium with which trustees were unfamiliar. Soon,
everyone knew about the changes in doctrinal policy and everyone in the
Convention was talking about them. And, of course, the debate over

whether or not they were best for our cooperative mission efforts was raised to a new level of participation.

It is possible that few would have paid attention to what I wrote on my blog were it not for the fact that readers, all of whom were probably Christians and most of whom were Southern Baptists, were given the ability to place uncensored comments on my blog. Some of the commentators were not exactly charitable and civil toward the IMB trustees, and some of the trustees wished to hold me accountable for comments that were not mine.[9] In fairness, other Southern Baptists made comments on my blog that lacked the characteristics of civility, not to mention Christian charity. The decision over whether I should censor such comments was not as easy as it might sound. The temptation for those of us who write on the Internet is to allow comments that support our positions and remove comments that offer an opposing view. I took the position, from the beginning, that I would not censor or remove any comment, friend or foe, unless cursing or vulgarities appeared in the comment.

This decision generated a great deal of discomfort for me, as it has others who have wrestled with the balance between freedom of speech and civility on the Internet. In 2007, *New York Times* columnist Brad Stone wrote an article titled "A Call for Manners in the World of Nasty Blogs." Stone tells the story of Kathy Sierra, a popular high-tech author who had advocated censoring impolitic and uncivil comments from Internet blogs.

A firestorm erupted in the insular community of dedicated technology bloggers. [Ms. Sierra became] distraught over the threats toward her and the manipulated photos of her that were posted on other sites critical of her recommendation—including one that depicted her head next to a noose. Ms. Sierra canceled a speaking appearance at a trade show and asked the local police for help in finding the source of the threats. She also said that she was considering giving up blogging altogether.

In an interview, she dismissed the argument that cyber bullying is so common that she should overlook it. "I can't believe how many people are saying to me, 'Get a life, this is the Internet,'" she said. "If that's the case, how will we ever recognize a real threat?"

Ms. Sierra said she supported the new efforts to improve civility on the Web. The police investigation into her case is pending. Menacing behavior is certainly not unique to the Internet. But since the Web offers the option of anonymity with no accountability, online conversations are often more prone to decay into ugliness than those in other media.[10]

When one considers that in 2008 there were well over 200 *million* blogs on the Internet, the accounts of uncivil behavior on the Internet should be both expected and numerous.[11] It is, however, another story for those sites that are Christian in nature. One would expect that Christians would seek, above all else, to model Christian charity and civility when they post writings on the Internet, but many Christians, intoxicated by the anonymity the Internet affords by being able to write either under a pseudonym or handle other than one's real name, often say things that would cause them to blush if associated with their names.

An illustration of such anonymity is seen in the establishment of church blogs dedicated to the undermining of pastoral leadership in many megachurches within the Southern Baptist Convention. Churches such as First Baptist Church, Jacksonville, Florida; Bellevue Baptist Church in Memphis, Tennessee; First Baptist Church, Dallas, Texas; and other large Southern Baptist churches have had to deal with anonymous bloggers who are dissatisfied with church leadership or direction. Additionally, LifeWay, the International Mission Board, and other Christian agencies within the Southern Baptist Convention, not to mention other evangelical denominations, have also struggled with blog sites established by anonymous people who are critical of administrative leadership. Ken Connor, chairman of the Center for a Just Society based in Washington, D.C., says of these anonymous writers, "[They are] nameless and faceless. They lurk in the shadows of many websites and blogs, waiting for any opportunity to tear those with whom they disagree to shreds."[12] The antithesis of true Christianity is darkness, concealment, and anonymity. I determined before I ever posted one article on the Internet that I would always publish under my name, place my e-mail address on the front page of my blog, and keep an open line of transparency and communication regarding anything I wrote. People who anonymously posted comments on my blog were usually the ones most uncivil, and I eventually came to the position that no anonymous comments would be allowed unless they were from missionaries living in Security Three zones and were unable, for security reasons, to identify themselves.

According to Scripture, backbiting is speaking in a *concealed manner* to ruin someone's good name. The Hebrew word translated "backbiting" means to "hide" or "conceal."[13] Thus, what Solomon calls "the backbiting tongue" is a euphemism for "hidden words intended to harm someone."[14] It is possible for a reputation to be stolen openly just as a robber can take something from you by an act of violence in a public square. But when someone steals

in secret, as when a Christian steals another's reputation by posting anonymous or "hidden" words, it reveals far more about the writer's character than
most people realize. David asked the question, "Lord, who shall abide in thy
tabernacle? Who shall dwell in thy holy hill?" The Lord answered, "He that
walks uprightly, and works righteousness, and speaks the truth in his heart
and he that backbites not."[15] The Scripture makes it clear that God's people
say what needs to be said *to the person to whom it needs to be said* before anything is said to anyone else.

This biblical understanding of backbiting, and my consternation with
seeing it violated by anonymous Internet posters and commenters, led me to
begin a journey to understand basic rules of Christian civility when writing
on or supervising comments for an Internet blog. On October 15, 2007, I
wrote a post titled "Christian Civility in an Uncivil World: A New Book" in
which I quoted a review of a book, *Uncommon Decency*, written by Christian
statesman Dr. Richard Mouw, president of Fuller Theological Seminary.[16]
The reviewer, Daniel B. Clendenin, writes of Mouw's book,

> Mouw shows how and why Christians should not only be people of con-
> viction, but people of compassion and civility. We are, he reminds us, to
> "pursue peace with everyone" (Hebrews 12:14), and to "show every cour-
> tesy to everyone" (Titus 3:2). Civility does not mean we have to like
> everyone we meet, forfeit our convictions to a relativistic perspective, or
> befriend people as a manipulative ploy to evangelize them. Rather, it means
> caring deeply about our civitas and its public life, because God so cares.
> After defining the nature and parameters of Christian civility, Mouw inves-
> tigates its implications for our speech, attitudes, pluralistic society, sexual
> mores, other religions, and leadership in a fallen world. He explores the
> limits of civility, when there is no "on the other hand." His chapter on hell
> asks whether we can believe in hell and still be civil. In his final two chap-
> ters he cautions against our tendencies to triumphalism, and trying to
> usher in the kingdom of God right now, as opposed to appreciating the
> ways and means of a patient, slow-moving God who loves His creation
> deeply and longs to redeem it.[17]

The last line of the review startled me. I have a high view of God's sover-
eignty, omnipotence, and authority, but I had never considered what the
reviewer calls "the slow-moving God." But of course, that is a good description of the way God works. The high-octane, speedy Internet has caught
Christians by surprise, and sometimes we seem to have raced ahead of a
"slow-moving God" in terms of what God intends for us in the realm of

Christian civility. In other words, too many of us Christians seem to be writing, posting, and commenting on the Internet for the entire world to see without asking whether or not the Spirit of God is in the midst of our writing.

I asked my readers to offer suggestions regarding rules for Christian civility on the Internet, and more than fifty different people responded. There were thoughtful responses, funny suggestions, and compelling rationales given for a set of rules that would guide the conduct of believers as they post their writings on the Internet. Compiling a summary of my readers' ideas, plus leaning upon the worthy *Blogger's Code of Conduct*[18] first published in 2007, I have sought to offer Ten Commandments for Christian Civility on the Internet. We Christians, above all others, have an extra incentive to reflect civility and humility, even when disagreements over principle cause conflict to arise. The ethic of Christ transcends the ethic of this world. Lord willing, this list of commands will be distributed far and wide to help ensure a greater degree of Christian civility on the Internet.

Ten Commandments for Christian Civility on the Internet

1. *We will seek to glorify God in all we write.* "So whether you eat or drink, or whatever you do, do all to the glory of God" (1 Cor 10:31). Nothing we write, no matter the content, can be called good without God's glory as the ultimate aim. If a person seeks recognition, his or her own praise, the applause of people, or any other selfish end through what he or she writes on the Internet, it should not be written, nor will it be accounted by God to be a good thing. There are no restrictions upon Paul's command, "Whatever you do, do all to the glory of God" (1 Cor 10:31). The best way to determine if God is glorified is to ask ourselves what God thinks about what we write. Is it God's will? Does it display God's attributes? Is it consistent with God's desires as expressed in the Bible? Does it honor God and God's people? Whether our words are formed for praise and prayers, concern and correction, exhortation and encouragement, they should glorify God first and foremost.

2. *We will refuse to post anything online that we wouldn't say face to face.* "The north wind brings forth rain, and a backbiting tongue, angry looks" (Prov 25:23). Unless we are in physical danger for what we would write or say, we will never write anonymously. Freedom of thought and freedom of expression are both human rights, and in those instances where governments, societies, or men seek to remove that right by force, we reserve the

right to post anonymously. Otherwise, we must be as responsible and civil on the Internet as we are in person. To hide behind anonymity on the Internet is similar to backbiting and gossiping, two serious sins. We will post it, claim it, and stand by it.

3. *When we are offended, we will connect privately before we respond publicly.* "If your brother sins against you, go and tell him his fault, between you and him alone" (Matt 18:15). There are times when posting differing philosophies, opinions, and thoughts will cause emotions to escalate. During these times, when offenses between brothers and sisters might occur, we will connect privately with the person with whom we have an offense before we write anything publicly. And we will keep in mind that Christian love covers a multitude of offenses.

4. *We will think carefully and pray sincerely, before we post.* "Let every person . . . be slow to speak" (Jas 1:19). Before we hit the submit button to publish our post, we will think twice about what we are trying to say and will ask ourselves "Is this how and what I really want to be conveyed?" Next, we will pause and ask God to give us wisdom and discernment, and reread the post for a final time. We will then ask if our words stand the test of eternity, when we shall give an account to God of everything we have said or written. If we prayerfully come to peace that what we have written honors God and advances God's kingdom, we will hit the submit button and publish our words.

5. *We will not allow others to corrupt our writing efforts.* "One who is wise is cautious and turns away from evil" (Prov 14:16). We are committed to enforce civility. We will strive for only acceptable content on our website, and we will delete all writing and comments that are unacceptable, such as (a) comments that are abusive, harassing, or threatening to others.
(b) comments we know are libelous and/or false.
(c) comments that infringe upon any copyright or trademark.
(d) comments that violate any obligation for confidentiality.
Though the above guidelines are often subjective, we determine what is unacceptable on a case-by-case basis, and our definitions are not limited to the above, but could grow as our knowledge and understanding of unacceptable content matures. When a comment or guest post is deleted, a clear explanation will always be given.

6. *We will not allow others to comment anonymously.*
Jesus said, "I have spoken openly. I have said nothing in secret" (John 18:20). We will require commenters to follow the example of Jesus and

supply their real first and last names, or if an alias or pseudonym is used, the commenter will supply to us a valid e-mail address with information about themselves before they can post. The necessity of an alias is only in rare circumstances (safety or security of the commenter), but we will always be able to trace the pseudonym to a real person.

7. *We will do no one any intentional harm.* "Therefore, encourage one another and build one another up" (1 Thess 5:11). We will intentionally seek to make the people around us better by writing things that encourage and build up. When times come that call for what we feel to be correction, we will speak the truth in love. We will never seek to destroy a reputation, harm a person's good name, or disparage a person's character. Our focus in writing will be on a person's conduct or actions, thinking or philosophy, but not character. The Spirit of God is able to change the heart, not us, and we will accept our brother or sister in Christ where the Lord has them in life.

8. *We will be decisive over what we delete.* "Was I vacillating when I wanted to do this? Do I make my plans according to the flesh, ready to say 'Yes, yes' and 'No, no' at the same time? Our word to you has not been Yes and No." (2 Cor 1:17-18) We have already stated the importance of taking responsibility for removing unacceptable material from our website. We retain the right to decide what is unacceptable and will not vacillate back and forth as those whose comments have been deleted argue and debate our decision.

9. *We will personally rebuke those who post unacceptable content.* "But when Peter came to Antioch, I rebuked him to his face" (Gal 2:11). When someone is publishing comments or blog postings that are offensive in nature, we will tell them privately if at all possible and prove, in writing, the unacceptability of what has been written. We will then ask them to make amends publicly, unless it is considered that doing so will only worsen the situation. Where published comments are considered threatening or libelous, we will involve local law enforcement. If the offensive material breaks no laws, and a private rebuke is not received, we will inform the public of the offense in order to create a civil online society where people feel the uncivilized are called out, just as they are in the real world. Of course, it is of highest importance that we safeguard the ability for people to feel safe in disagreement, and that rebukes never be used to silence dissent. Rebukes are used as a last resort only for those who are uncivilized in their writing.

10. *We will promote these commandments for increased online Christian civility.* "I appeal to you, brothers, to watch out for those who cause divisions

and create obstacles contrary to the doctrine that you have been taught" (Rom 16:17). We appeal to all our Christian brothers who write or read published Internet postings to distribute and promote these commandments for Christian civility on the Internet. Through raising awareness of particular actions that can be taken to ensure civility, we "watch out for those who cause divisions."

One might find it odd that the man who caused such displeasure with what he published on the Internet is the person who writes Ten Commandments for Christian Civility on the Internet. I am confident, however, that after a thorough reading of any and all of my 700 published online postings, the impartial reader will see that they did not deviate from these commandments. It remains my duty to maintain civility and Christian decorum toward all, and as I continue to post via the Internet, Christian civility remains my aim.

Notes

1. Claudia Roden, *Book of Middle Eastern Food* (New York: Vintage Publisher, 1974) 49.

2. Matthew 22:35-40.

3. Moncure D. Conway, *George Washington's Rules of Civility: Traced to Their Sources* (New York: United States Book Company, 1890) 180.

4. Wade Burleson, *Grace and Truth to You*, http://www.kerussocharis.com (December 2005).

5. Wade Burleson, "To My Friends, Family, Church, and the Southern Baptist Convention," http://kerussocharis.blogspot.com/2006/01/to-my-friends-family-church-and.html, 11 January 2006.

6. Wade Burleson, "Decisions," http://kerussocharis.blogspot.com/2006/03/decisions.html, 22 March 2006.

7. George F. Will, "The Last Word," *Newsweek*, 7 July 1997.

8. Terrence Crawford, *10 Commandments for Board Members*, 1981, as cited by the New Jersey Law Blog, http://www.njlawblog.com/2007/06/articles/community-associations/10-commandments-for-board-members-revisited/, 6 June 2007.

9. Wade Burleson, "Five Salient Points," http://kerussocharis.blogspot.com/2006/01/five-salient-points.html, 14 January 2006.

10. Brad Stone, "A Call for Manners in the World of Nasty Blogs," *New York Times*, 9 April 2007.

11. "How Many Blogs Are There on the Internet?" *The Blog Herald*, http://www.blogherald.com/2008/02/11/how-many-blogs-are-there-is-someone-still-counting/, 11 February 2008.

12. Ken Connor, "Online Anger Undermines Discourse," Baptist Press, http://www.bpnews.net/BPFirstPerson.asp?ID=26077, 16 July 2007.

13. Proverbs 25:23.

14. Ibid.

15. Psalm 15:1-3a.

16. Wade Burleson, "Christian Civility in an Unchristian World: A New Book," http://kerussocharis. blogspot.com/2007/10/christian-civility-in-in-uncivil-world-new.html, 15 October 2007.

17. Ibid.

18. "Blogger's Code of Conduct," Blogging Wikia, http://www.blogging.wikia.com.

Chapter 8

The Power of Words

Mitch Carnell,
Consultant, Speaker, Writer

Prayer: "O God, who wants all men to live together on the earth, make me careful to avoid all that can break the cord that unites me with other men. Regulate all my words and all my actions so that they may be agreeable to my brothers. Do not allow me by uncivil and rude conduct to attract their hatred and contempt. But also do not allow me to offend You while trying to please them. Cause me above everything else to think about how I might make myself agreeable in Your eyes in order one day to rejoice in Your glory. Amen."[1]

Carol, my wife, taught in an inner-city middle school in 2005, and I volunteered to help some of the students with their writing skills. I was overwhelmed by the pervasive nature of negativity from both the students and the faculty. I felt that someone had to do something. One day the principal told the students, "If you want to do well this year, just be nice." An idea struck me. I wrote a little booklet titled *Say Something Nice: Be a Lifter.* My goal was for those in public and private schools to use it, but that didn't happen. The city of North Charleston was interested, though. The city bought copies for its employees. The city of Charleston bought copies for its neighborhood presidents and invited me to conduct a workshop on the topic. Mayor Keith Summey of North Charleston declared the first Say Something Nice Day on June 1, 2006.

In the meantime, the rhetoric in the Christian community went from bad to worse. All the major denominations are now on the brink of splintering. Some groups have taken out full-page newspaper ads denouncing each other.

Dr. Frank Page was elected as president of the Southern Baptist Convention in 2006 because he argued convincingly for turning down the dialogue that has disrupted the Convention for more than thirty years. Mainly due to the Internet, he was elected by the rank and file in spite of the presence of candidates favored and strongly supported by the entrenched leadership. Dr. Page is no less conservative than those he defeated, but he advocates for a more respectful climate. The presiding bishop of the Episcopal Church, Katharine Schori, has argued the same position, and the United Methodist Church has adopted a policy on "Holy Conferencing" as a procedure designed to help keep discussions in bounds and distinctly Christian.

The First Baptist Church of Charleston, South Carolina, the oldest Baptist congregation in the South, became so concerned about the deplorable state of Christian discourse that it set aside the first Sunday in June of each year as Say Something Nice Sunday. The congregation realized the need for at least a pause in poisonous rhetoric. The Charleston Baptist Association and the Charleston Atlantic Presbytery joined the effort, as did the Cooperative Baptist Fellowship of South Carolina. The South Carolina Baptist Convention passed a resolution supporting the program "Unity in the Body." This modest effort drew strong criticism from some of the fundamentalist groups that felt we were watering down the gospel. Even an attempt to say nice things about other Christian groups puts you at odds with some groups that favor a more militant type of evangelism. The appearance of Tony Campolo as a speaker for the Hamrick Lectures in 2007 brought even more criticism. First Baptist Charleston has a long history of inviting speakers with diverse points of view to address the congregation and the community. This commitment appears in the covenant of the church adopted by the congregation on August 21, 1791: "We will be careful to conduct ourselves with uprightness and integrity, and in a peaceful and friendly manner, toward mankind in general, and toward Christians of all descriptions, in particular." The Hamrick Lectures represent a rebirth of that tradition. The current pastor, the Reverend Marshall Blalock, answered the criticism with great grace by simply stating, "The members of First Baptist Church are sophisticated enough to decide for themselves."

Martin Marty, writing in his foreword to Quentin J. Schultze's book, *Communicating for Life*, recalls the time when he shared a platform with theologian Joseph Sittler, who had become blind. Sittler was asked to explain in as few words as possible his vision for church reform. "Watch your language," Sittler said. Marty goes on to explain, "Watch your language and you will learn how to confront what is dehumanizing and demeaning in others."[2] FBC Charleston's Marshall Blalock passed that test with flying colors with his response to the criticism.

The second celebration of Say Something Nice Sunday on June 1, 2008, drew this response from James B. Smith, executive editor of the *Florida Baptist Witness*, in an editorial, "Gospel-free Sunday": "Niceness is breaking out in South Carolina Baptist Churches. I pray the rest of the Southern Baptist Convention is not next."[3] Don Kirkland, editor of the *South Carolina Baptist Courier*, asked Blalock if he wished to respond to the criticism. The Reverend Blalock answered, "No. The editorial speaks for itself." Many negative blog posts on the Internet derided the proposition that Christians should be nice to one another.

"Sticks and stones may break my bones but words can never hurt me." Nothing could be further from the truth than this folk saying. While broken bones mend and bruises eventually fade, the damage done with unkind words often lasts a lifetime. Words once spoken take on a life of their own. No matter how repentant we are, we can never recall harmful words. Schultze reasons, "Whenever we communicate peacefully in accordance with God, we taste heaven." Ken Connor, president of the Center for a Just Society in Washington, D.C., titled a column he wrote, "Words Really Do Matter."[4]

Words are the vehicles through which we transmit ideas, and since ideas have consequences, words have consequences. Words shape our beliefs, and what we believe determines how we behave. Therefore, words inspire behavior. Mark Twain understood this when he said, "The difference between the right word and the almost right word is like the difference between lightning and the lightning bug."

The words of the Declaration of Independence inspired people to give their lives in pursuit of the ideas embodied in it. Abraham Lincoln changed the course of history when he wrote the Emancipation Proclamation. Martin Luther King's oratory inspired the nation finally to live up to the ideals of its founding. Edward R. Murrow, in lionizing Winston Churchill, said he "mobilized the English language and sent it into battle."

Words are not empty vessels. They are pregnant with meaning and laden with content. They evoke images and transmit feelings. They can hurt or heal and cause anger or heartache or comfort. The writer of Ephesians understood this when he adjured his readers, "Do not let any unwholesome talk come out of your mouths, but only what is helpful for building others up according to their needs, that it may benefit those who listen" (Eph 4:29 NIV). The writer of Proverbs acknowledged that words have impact when he wrote, "Reckless words pierce like a sword, but the tongue of the wise brings healing" (Prov 12:18 NIV).

Once, I conducted a workshop for faculty members at a local college, and we discussed the impact of words on our relationships. Each person there recalled a remark made by a parent when he or she was young that continues to haunt that person. Slowly and painfully each individual recalled the event and the hurtful words. It was clear that those words had taken a terrible toll. Some of the injuries were more than forty years old; however, they were as fresh and as painful as the day the words were spoken. It was difficult to listen to their hurts and to see the pain in their faces.

I had not seen my college friend John in fifty years until our reunion at Mars Hill College, but John recalled verbatim a slashing remark I had made to him when we were on opposite sides in a college debate. The remark, even though it was not personal, was devastating nevertheless. My friend Tom still hurts from a cutting remark I made to him forty years ago after one of our state speech and hearing association meetings. Though remorseful and ashamed of my behavior, I cannot erase those words. At the time I thought they were clever, but time has shown that they were not received that way. They caused hurt.

The words of Senator Lloyd Bentsen to Dan Quayle during the vice presidential debates in 1988 in Omaha, Nebraska, which were carried on national television, are seared into the nation's consciousness. Quayle had compared his experience to that of John Kennedy. Turning to face Quayle, Senator Bentsen said, "Senator, I served with Jack Kennedy. I knew Jack Kennedy. Jack Kennedy was a friend of mine. Senator, you're no John Kennedy." No matter which side of the political spectrum those who heard the remark were on, those words cut to the quick. They are still used in various forms even today.

Just as words have the power to hurt, they also have the power to build up, to comfort, and to inspire. The words of Franklin Delano Roosevelt inspired a nation gripped by a great depression: "The only thing we have to fear is fear itself." Who can measure the effect of the words of Winston Churchill to the British during the Second World War? "Never give in. Never, Never, Never." John Kennedy spurred a nation toward great achievement with his words, "Ask not what your country can do for you; ask what you can do for your country." Think of the power generated by the words of Martin Luther King, Jr.: "Free at last. Free at last. Thank God almighty. I'm free at last."

It was near midnight on Seabrook Island near Charleston. The late Sam Lyons and I were the only two white people at a meeting sponsored by the

Sea Island Comprehensive Health Commission. There were twenty or thirty African Americans present. We finished the meeting by joining hands in a circle and singing the great hymn of the civil rights movement, "We Shall Overcome." "Deep in my heart I do believe that we shall overcome some-day." Words can never express the effect this moment had on me. Yes, the setting played a great part in the power of that moment, but those words carried an immense message to my heart. After that experience, I could never return to a place of cool indifference.

In November 1993, I found myself in the Crystal Cathedral in California along with my friends Tom and Vickie Guerry and their son Benjamin. I was still in deep mourning for my wife of thirty-two years, who had died in 1989. During his sermon, Robert Schuler said, "Don't count what you have lost. Count what you have left." I thought of my two wonderful children, my grandson, my sister, my friends, my church, and my work. When I returned home, I began to make a list of my blessings. I added to that list every day until I realized there were so many blessings that I could not count them all. As I read and reread the list daily, I gained strength and courage. "Count your many blessings. Name them one by one. Count your many blessings. See what God has done."[5] I dare you to try this simple exercise. I am forever grateful to Dr. Schuler for those words. I am sure I had heard them before, but at that moment I was receptive. The words took root deep in my soul. At my wife's funeral, Dr. Scott Walker in his eulogy painted a picture of the God I believe in when he said, "When that aneurism struck Liz, God was the first to cry." Those words say that we have a compassionate God who cares deeply about each one of us. Can you think of a better way to say that God is love?

When Liz was in a coma in ICU, friends kept me company every day. One night I confessed to my friends Anne and Gill Pooser that I didn't know what to pray for. I wanted desperately for her to live, but I also knew that her life would be in name only. Anne, a member of the Sunday school class I taught, said, "Mitch, you don't have to know. God knows what is in your heart and the Spirit prays for you." Then she quoted that magnificent Scripture: "Likewise the Spirit helps us in our weakness; for we do not know how to pray as we ought, but the Spirit himself intercedes for us with sighs too deep for words."[6]

Words carry the power to comfort. I had developed a case of Bell's palsy, although at the time I did not know what it was. I thought my career was over. I went for an appointment with Dr. Willy Schwenzfeier. Dr. Willy pulled up a chair and put his hand on my knee and said, "Mitch, I know that you are scared. Let me show you what has happened." He drew the path of the facial nerve on a chart explaining about Bell's palsy. Then he said, "The next three weeks will be the most miserable three weeks you have ever spent, but then you will be all right." I walked out of his office a different person. The doctor I had seen the previous weekend in an emergency center could have told me the same thing, but he didn't. He left me consumed by my fear when a few words would have soothed my jagged nerves. Words are powerful, whether they are spoken thoughtlessly or unspoken when desperately needed.

Each of us carries the power to heal, to reassure, to console, to encourage. Our words have the power to transform lives. My dad was not one for sentimentality, but my sister, Jean, and I planned a celebration for our parents' fiftieth anniversary at Antioch Baptist Church. Mother was already deep in the throes of Alzheimer's disease, and it was all she could do to be present. I am sure she had no idea what was taking place. She sat at the table and smiled as the guests greeted her. One of the guests said to dad, "Claude, fifty years is a long time, isn't it?" Dad's response revealed a side of him that rarely surfaced. "Not nearly long enough," he said quietly. That moment is precious to me. What more needs to be said? He could make that statement even when his wife and soul mate of fifty years did not know who he was or how important he was to her. He was not grandstanding. It was a simple remark made to one individual, but I was blessed to hear it.

When I conduct workshops dealing with interpersonal communication, I often use a simple exercise involving words. I ask participants to list the most beautiful words they know, and the softest, the ugliest, and the meanest. Beautiful words and soft words are often difficult to pull out of the attendees. They struggle with those; however, ugly and mean words pour out in torrents. In addition, the attendees frequently whisper to one another words they consider too inappropriate for a public forum. They need no encouragement for this part of the exercise. Why are we so conditioned to utter and accept negative comments? I called my friend to tell him how good the choir sounded at church. "Yes, but the choir was thin—too many people absent." "We really had great attendance in the congregation today," I said. "Yes, there were a lot of visitors," he replied.

When my graduate students make oral presentations, my rule is that the presenter must tell me what he or she likes about the presentation before saying anything negative. It is a difficult requirement because almost without exception each presenter starts to critique herself or himself with something negative. "I should have . . . ," "It would have been better if I had . . . ," and the list goes on. "No," I say. "Tell me something that you did right." The presenter often struggles to find something positive to say. At times I even have to prompt the person with questions before he or she can say something positive. Did you know your subject matter? Were you prepared? Did you find the topic interesting?

The psalmist certainly got it right. There is an unbroken link between what we think and what we say. "Let the words of my mouth and the meditation of my heart be acceptable . . ."(Ps 19:14). When we dwell on negative thoughts, it is only natural for those thoughts to find verbal expression. After one of my columns appeared in the *Business Review* magazine (published by the *Charleston Post and Courier*), discussing the negativity that surrounds us and how it is so contagious, one of my friends called to chide me. "Mitch, we can't be positive all the time." Of course, there are things we need to correct. There are aspects of our daily existence that we should work to improve. My point is that we need to keep these in perspective.

Looking back on these events in my life is often painful. After he was an adult, my son told me, "Dad, you never told me I did a good job cleaning my room. You always said, 'It looks better. You're getting there.' You never said, 'Son, you did a great job.'" I am not proud of that. It is painful to realize that I withheld the praise he deserved and needed so badly. Yes, I had my reasons. I did not want to let him think that his room was now perfect or that there was not room for improvement. I can justify my behavior in my own mind, but not in my son's. I should have realized this because the highest praise I could get from my own father was, "It'll do."

Where does this demand for perfection come from? Our heavenly Father doesn't require us to be perfect before he rescues us. My son has mastered an attitude that neither I nor my father demonstrated. In speaking of his own son, my grandson, he said, "Dad, I can't come down on him about this grade. He has already beaten up on himself about it." Wow! He gets it. What love! What an understanding father. Mike has broken the chain of well-intended but half-hearted praise. Mike is not a good father; he is a great father.

Mike's mother got it right. She taught three-year-old preschool. One day a little boy was upset because all of his playmates had superhero character underwear and his was stark white. "You have superhero underwear," she told the distraught child. "You're the Iceman." He went off happy as can be.

Am I saying that anything goes? No, of course not. What I am saying is that we need to keep minor things minor. Our first rule should be the same as that in the medical profession—do no harm. Do nothing that would worsen an already bad situation. My police officer friends tell me there are certain officers with whom you do not want to work a crime scene because they make the situation worse. I have heard the same story from firefighters. It is always easier to escalate a situation than it is to deescalate one. "A soft answer turneth away wrath" (Prov 15:1).

When a situation needs to be addressed and you are the appropriate one to address it, do it directly. State your expectations for correction. Make certain that you have been clearly understood. Then leave it alone.

The Bible is clear: "So when you are offering your gift at the altar, if you remember that your brother or sister has something against you, leave your gift there before the altar and go; first be reconciled to your brother or sister, and then come and offer your gift."[7] In other words, come to the altar with a clean heart. Only then are we to make our offering. God is interested in what is on the inside.

A good friend and fellow church member was writing inflammatory letters to our pastor. The situation reached a dangerous point. As chair of the diaconate, I invited him to a meeting with two other deacons. We gave him an opportunity to express his concerns. I then explained that he had every right to express his concerns and that we would address them. We went further to tell him that the way in which he expressed his displeasure was unacceptable, and we wanted him to agree to stop writing the abusive letters. He agreed that he had gone too far and that he would not write more letters. We assured him that he is a valuable member of the congregation with many talents and that there is an appropriate way to express concerns and disagreements. We assured him that either one of the three of us would be willing to go with him to address a specific matter if he felt he was not being heard.

It was a successful meeting with all parties feeling good about what happened. He has kept his word. There have been no more letters, he is a valuable contributing member of the church, and we have remained friends. I could not have led this process without first praying about it and asking for guidance. I then had to get my emotions straight so that I could approach the matter in a calm, nonjudgmental way. In a congregational church, everyone has a right to express his or her opinion, but no one has the right to abuse another person in the process. As Christians, we are obligated to guard our speech and to use it to build up the fellowship.

This incident is mild in comparison to what happened to a friend who is a minister in a different denomination. Several members of his congregation mounted a vicious letter-writing campaign against him in order to get him removed. The letter writers resorted to gross misstatements of facts and spread rumors of gigantic proportion. He asked me to read these in order to help him gain perspective; we are friends and he knew that I would pray about the situation. The letter writers were eventually unsuccessful because wiser people in the congregation prevailed. They knew they had a minister of tremendous talent who worked tirelessly on their behalf and who dedicated himself to pastoral care, prayer, and Bible study. Nevertheless, this situation caused great harm to the local church and to many people on both sides. It could have been avoided if the members had communicated in such a way that would solve the problems and honor Christ in the process.

We do not often pass the peace in our worship services. When we do, it sometimes tends to get out of hand. Some members have objected to the practice on this basis. It occurred to me that as hard as we try not to let it happen, some people could come and go away from a service without being touched or even spoken to. Ours is a friendly, compassionate congregation, but such disconnection could happen. This may be the only time the worshiper has contact with another person all week. A little disorder is greatly outweighed by the possible good. Being kind and considerate never goes out of style. I know this can happen because I have been the visitor in other congregations and was not greeted. It is a lonely feeling. Of course, I could have changed that by speaking to someone myself. I am a fairly talkative person, and if I let myself be ignored, think of the person who is shy and withdrawn. We need to be connected. Think of the comfort and the hope these simple words convey: "May the peace of Christ be with you." Saying these words while grasping the hand of another believer will take you through a lonely week.

The Christian community is diverse. Even individual congregations may contain many different races, nationalities, beliefs, levels of understanding, and degrees of commitment. How each worshiper is treated is a matter of great concern. Think about the variety of churches and denominations in the United States and try to comprehend the variety worldwide. It is impossible for us to conceive. What we know is that there is some similarity but little uniformity even in liturgical churches.

Of course, we differ on many issues, but we also agree on far more. How are we to treat our brothers and sisters in Christ? Once again, we turn to the

Bible for guidance: "I give you a new commandment, that you love one another. Just as I have loved you, you should also love one another. By this everyone will know that you are my disciples, if you have love for one another."[6] Love is the key. I am not required to agree with you or even to like you. I am required to respect you. I cannot love the Creator and hate creation. You are God's handiwork. You are God's crowning achievement on earth. You are created in God's own image.

This is often a heavy burden. It is easy to disparage another group, to ridicule or simply to discount them. The Bible tells us that we ourselves were once strangers. Quentin Schultze has it right: "Love is not just a feeling or emotion but wisdom and passion garnered ultimately from the Creator. Loving God through our communication takes a great deal of hard work, serious study, wise discernment and lifelong practice."[9]

In their book, *The Complete Book of Everyday Christianity*, Robert Banks and Paul Stevens tell us,

> Civility is not a biblical term as such, but the idea is certainly present in the Scriptures. Indeed, taken as a way of describing respect for strangers, civility is a rather prominent motif. In the Old Testament God regularly encourages the people of Israel to show courtesy to those who were different from themselves, For example, the chosen people are reminded that they received God's mercy even when they were still strangers: "For you were aliens in the land of Egypt" (Leviticus 19:34). This theme is repeated in the New Testament: Christians are called to "speak evil of no one, to avoid quarreling, to be gentle, and to show courtesy to everyone." (Titus 3:2 NRSV).[10]

Wes White has translated some of the writings of Benedict Pictet and writes, "In order for our civility to be truly Christian it must be founded in a principle of charity and love of our neighbor."[11]

Although we have separated ourselves into numerous divisions, we are all members of one great family. There is only one God who created us all. Since faith is based on believing, not knowing, why do we become so upset with each other? Often the answer is fear. We fear what we do not know or understand. How often are we told in the Scriptures to "Fear not"? Much of our hostile language is the language of fear. We try to make ourselves secure by attacking with our words. This behavior is unacceptable to God and destroys our witness. Why would nonbelievers want to be like us if there is no difference in our behavior and that of those who don't believe? If my goal is to point you to a life in Christ, then I must at the very least try to model Christ in my actions toward you. That includes my speech.

We need to look no further than Genesis 1:3 to see the power of words. "God said, 'let there be light' and there was light." Our speech is a gift from God. We should think of our speech as a sacred trust. With it we have the power to create beauty, wholeness, and relationships, but with it we also have the power to destroy. "Let your bodies be a living sacrifice, wholly committed unto God" (Rom 12:1). It is not far into the creation story that man becomes a co-creator with God through speech. God gives to Adam the responsibility of naming all the inhabitants of creation. Adam gives the creatures their names. This is important because in the ancient world, to know the name of something was to have some control over it. We see this even in today's world. Name calling has always been a major factor in bullying and making fun of other children. Sadly, this carries over into adulthood and the workplace and religious life as evidenced by terms such as scabs, lintheads, slackers, suck ups, mackerel snappers, whiskypalians, Bible thumpers, holy rollers. Even "Christian" was often used as a derogatory term, and today "evangelical" carries a negative connotation.

Several years ago the South Carolina Marine Resources Commission created a program to get people to eat different kinds of fish. Some of the fish had terrible off-putting names. The experiment was to have people taste fish with these names without knowing the name of the fish sampled. People who previously would not eat that fish because of its name now had a favorable reaction to the same fish. In church circles today, congregations are opting to omit the denominational name in order to attract members because the denominational names have become associated with negative judgmental theology. For example, there is Carolina Community Church, which in reality is a Southern Baptist church. What started as the Baptist College of Charleston, South Carolina, is now Charleston Southern University because marketing research showed that putting the denomination's label on the institution was a deterrent to prospective students and fund-raising, even though the institution is closely aligned with and supported by the South Carolina Baptist Convention.

We all can attest to the healing, uplifting power of words. Kind words can work magic. Why are we so reluctant to speak the words that others desperately need to hear? We have the power to change another person's day by simply speaking kind words. "I forgive you. I love you. Come home. I'm glad to see you. Thank you. You are a good teacher. I'm glad you're my friend. I missed you. You did a great job. I enjoy your company. You can do it. I'll go with you. Take my hand. Welcome. Your presence makes such a difference. You belong here. You are among friends. God bless you. I am praying for you."

Words are far too powerful to be thrown about casually. They are the building blocks of all our relationships. We can use them to build a bridge between one another or to erect walls that none of us can penetrate. My prayer is for the bridges.

Marlo Thomas has written a terrific book, *The Right Word at the Right Time* (Atria Books, 2002). I recommend her book to everyone, but you do not need to read her book to know the power of words. In high school, I wanted desperately to fit in. I developed a terrible habit of holding back in history class even though I knew the answer to the question. When I was called on, I prefaced my answer with, "I guess." One day Mrs. Pearson, who instilled a love of history in hundreds of students, said to me, "Mitch, you are not guessing. You know the answer. Answer the question."

I have been active in church and church programs since I was a toddler. Perhaps the most meaningful, life-changing, freeing words ever spoken to me came from a minister serving a cotton mill village church in upper South Carolina. At the time, I was in elementary school. I had no idea then what a gift Mr. Gowan was giving me. "Mitchell," he said, "God made all of you, and that includes your brain. He did not expect you to park it at the door when you come to church." Wow! It took me years to comprehend the full impact of those words, but they have had a profound effect on my life. That congregation nourished me and gave me a solid foundation to face the world.

It was also there that I first learned that church members are not always generous with their language. One Sunday morning a member stood to give a visitation report, but instead of reciting the number of visits and results, he said, "When I visited this one house, the resident wanted to know why the minister wasn't doing the visiting." His remarks were intended to wound. A deafening silence followed. My dad later expressed his anger to me about what the member had said. Ministers lead a difficult life. I visited in the home of Preacher Gowan while I was still in elementary school. Mrs. Gowan directed me to his study. There he was, leaning over a radio. "What are you listening to?" I asked. "The World Series," he replied. "Well, turn it up so we can hear it," I said. "No," he said. "If I did that, some church member would come into the parlor and hear it and want to know why I wasn't out visiting the sick." Since that time I have been keenly aware of the fishbowl that most members of the cloth inhabit.

The Tyranny of Gossip

Gossip exacts a terrible penalty. Years after this incident and in another church, rumors circulated that a close minister friend did not believe certain parts of the Bible. The truth is that he was a serious biblical scholar. However, no amount of reasoning could quell the rumors. This terrible state of affairs contributed to an eventual church split. Gossip is the most destructive force in most churches today, as it is in the workplace and society in general.

How does one deal with such a situation? Cut it off at the source. I interviewed a young woman for a position at the Charleston Speech and Hearing Center, and she did not get the job. In her frustration, she telephoned one of the members of the board of directors and complained that I had been rude to her. The board member told me how she had responded to the woman. "I told her that I knew you and that you may have disagreed with her, but said, 'Dr. Carnell was not rude to you.'" Wow! That is how to stop gossip. Confront it. Do not listen to it and refuse to pass it along. A good response is to say, "If you don't want anyone else to know this, you had better not tell me. I can keep a secret, but I have too many friends who cannot." Gossip hurts three people: the person that it is about, the person who listens, and the person who spreads it.

A wonderful ancient story told by Rabbi Joseph Telushkin in his book *Words That Hurt; Words That Heal* concerns a rabbi who had been the victim of gossip. Finally the gossiper came to the rabbi to ask forgiveness. The rabbi told him to cut open a pillow and allow the wind to scatter the feathers. After doing this, the man returned to the rabbi. The rabbi told him, "Go pick up all of the feathers." "This is impossible," said the guilt-stricken man. "So it is with your words. They cannot be recalled," said the rabbi.[12]

Words are powerful beyond our wildest expectations. When our daughter, Suzanne, was three, she developed a terrible case of croup. Even though we lived in a second-floor apartment, I could hear her awful cough when I got out of the car that night. We constructed a tent and put a cold steam vaporizer inside. I held her all night inside the tent. When she experienced a wrenching cough that tore my heart out, she gripped me tightly and said, "I love you, Daddy." Even today, we never part company or end a telephone call without those magic words. They are part of the unbreakable bond between us.

Liz, my late wife, had a wonderful way with words. She is the only person I have ever known who actually used the word "balderdash." Sometimes when I would tell her that a word didn't mean what she thought it did, she would say, "It does if I pay it enough." It was her way of reminding me that the meaning of a word is unique to each person. It is true that the dictionary gives us the common or most appropriate meaning, but the real meaning of words lies in the nervous system of each individual. Naturally, this is also often the cause of many hurt feelings. We need to make certain that our words accurately transmit our meaning.

Words Have Influence

Of all the names by which Jesus is known, my favorite is Emmanuel—God with us. The comfort it brings in my mind is reassuring. To me it means that wherever I am or whatever the circumstances, I am not alone. God is with me. Running a close second is Prince of Peace. Here I find calmness and absence of strife, but peace is so much more. It means wholeness, assurance, completeness. Let yourself feel the effects of the words. Clear your mind and let the words saunter through your awareness. Words have a way of making themselves part of the fabric of our lives.

My mother loved Tennyson's "Crossing the Bar." If I close my eyes I can hear her reciting it to me often when I helped her with the dishes: "Sunset and evening star, And one clear call for me! And may there be no moaning at the bar, when I put out to sea." Then there came the lines of that magnificent last verse: "I hope to see my Pilot face to face when I have crossed the bar."[13] These words bring comfort and peace to me because they did for her. Mother loved life, but she loved God even more. She did not fear death and neither do I. When I first heard those words, I didn't have a clue as to their meaning; I only knew my mother loved them. Now they give me comfort and assurance because I know that she has met her Pilot face to face, and one day I will share that experience. Carol, my wife, said to me one day, "You just think of heaven as some place you haven't been."

Our language is a sacred trust. With it we can join God in the act of creating a world fit to dwell in. We can lift people up and help them become what God intended for them to be. With our words we can also be a mighty force for evil, destroying other people's lives as well as our own. In the wonderful book, *How Full Is Your Bucket?* (Gallop, 2004), authors Tom Rath and

Donald O. Clifton use the analogy of a bucket to illustrate the point that each of us carries with us a bucket that can be filled or emptied by positive or negative words. When I dip out of your bucket with hurtful words, I also dip out of mine. Words once spoken can never be recalled. Their sword can never be resheathed. God has trusted us with a powerful force to be used for good or evil. He has given us free will; therefore, the choice is ours. I have often fallen for the cheap shot and gone for laughs, not realizing the damage I inflicted. There is a better way, a higher ground. The psalmist spells it out for us: "Let the words of my mouth and the meditation of my heart be acceptable in thy sight, O LORD, my strength and my redeemer."[14]

Words can destroy relationships. Sometimes our words are heard in a way far different from what we intended. We have no way to know the state of mind or emotional health of our hearer at the moment. Dr. Arthur Caliandro, former pastor of Marble Collegiate Church in New York City, writes in his book, *Make Your Life Count,*

> People might not always respond to me as I would like, but I can decide how I will respond to them. This is what Jesus spoke about when he preached his most challenging and exciting sermon. I don't always feel like loving others. I don't always feel like being forgiving. It is often easier to judge and often there is an evil pleasure in carrying resentments. Jesus understood these feelings. Yet he also understood the necessity of taking charge of self and rising above them. Jesus spoke directly to each of us when he commanded us to love one another.[15]

In 1983, I was fortunate to be chosen to attend the Community Executive Program sponsored by IBM. The program was part of the company's response to President Reagan's call for private industry to become involved in the not-for-profit movement. The purpose of the program was to expose leaders in not-for-profit agencies to the latest business theories and practices so that we might incorporate them into our programs back home. The workshop took place at the IBM Conference Center in Tarrytown, New York. There were twenty-three of us from all over the United States. It was easily the most helpful, most stimulating, and most productive program I have ever attended. I continue to use most of what I learned there.

There was much that awed me, but the speaker who impressed me more than all the others had a simple message. He impressed me because it was not what I had expected to hear and because it came from IBM, perhaps the most successful company on earth at that time. Certainly, one could depend

on it for sound business advice. IBM was so serious about this week of training that it did not provide any alcoholic beverages during the seminar. What
was that advice from one of the world's most respected companies?

> During the year that is ending or during the past several years, you have
> lost a good friend due to a misunderstanding. The details have now
> become so clouded that you no longer know what it was all about or who
> said what to whom. You only know that you have lost a friend. It no longer
> matters who was at fault. Your assignment for tonight before you go to bed
> is to call that person. You tell him or her that you are sorry for your part in
> the disagreement and that you would like to rekindle your friendship. Do
> it as soon as you are dismissed from this session.

I looked about me. I wasn't in church. I wasn't even at a United Way
meeting. I was at the IBM Conference Center. It wasn't Christmas; it was
mid-August. This advice, directive, was coming from a company known for
its profit-making. The company was putting people ahead of everything else.
What was he really saying? Get your priorities straight. People are the most
important element in any business, either for-profit or not-for-profit. Take
responsibility for what you do. Apologize for your part in the disagreement.
Don't blame it on somebody else. Don't hide behind circumstances. Take
responsibility. Act now. Don't wait for a more convenient time. There isn't
one. Offer a plan. I want to rekindle our friendship. The phone call will no
doubt lead to an awkward moment in which all could be lost. Don't allow
that to happen. Seize the moment. You may be able to undo the wounds that
hurtful words have inflicted or at least start the healing process.

All of us know that words are more than symbols on a page or sound
waves that stir the air. They have power for building up or tearing down. We
want our words to mirror the image of the One who came to save us. Our
speech is a sacred trust.

Active Listening Is Essential

How often have you been talking with someone only to realize that his or
her mind is somewhere else? He or she is not listening to you. We Americans
are poor listeners. We are accustomed to getting our information in sound
bites. The great oral tradition of the past is all but gone. Our failure to listen
accounts for much of our failed communication. Certainly we must choose
our words wisely, but of equal importance is to listen to the other person
attentively. There are many distractions in our daily lives that we must

combat in order to listen. Today we are confronted not only with the telephone, radio, and television, but also with cell phones, text messaging,
e-mail, and countless other digital distractions.

Often we are so busy framing what we want to say if and when the other
person stops talking or at least takes a breath that we miss his or her meaning
entirely. We hear the words but we miss the subtle cues to the deeper meaning. We have hot buttons, and when they are pushed we become emotional
and lose our ability to think logically. This is important everywhere, but
often in religious conversations it becomes more acute. We easily take offense
when the other person's views do not mirror our own. Unfortunately, many
of us have not grown in our understanding of Scripture since our early days
as a believer. We stubbornly cling to our earlier beliefs or attitudes without
further examination. Many of us refuse to listen to those whose viewpoints
differ from our own. As our society grows more and more pluralistic, it
becomes essential to listen to others just as we want others to listen to our
testimony. I am in no way implying that one should give up deeply held convictions on matters of substance, but only that we listen with open hearts as
well as open minds.

We receive little training in school or in church on how to listen. Our
only training usually is embodied in a threat. You had better listen. You are
going to need this. For this reason I developed a pledge to help improve the
quality of listening, "My Covenant for Improved Communication."

> I will listen to you without interruption for at least two minutes. I will look
> at you while you are talking and not engage in any other activity. When I
> do respond to you, I will respond appropriately to what you said. I will not
> pin a label on you or call you names. I will not raise my voice or use pro-
> fanity. I will keep my remarks centered in the present and not dredge up
> the past. I will treat you with the same respect that I demand for myself.[16]

Those who have used this covenant tell me it works, although it takes
time to reach two minutes without talking. Remember that just because you
stop talking does not mean you are listening. Listening requires work and
concentration. The keys to civility in our communication require restraint
with our language, careful and thoughtful choice of words, active listening,
and an attitude that says I care about you. You are important to me. Our
communication as Christians, whether speaking, listening, or writing, is
rooted in the commandment of Jesus that we love one another. "Kind words
can be short and easy to use, but their echoes are truly endless."[17]

Notes

1. Benedict Pictet, *La Morale Chrestienne*, vol. 6., trans. (from French) Wes White, http://Johannesw2slianus. blogspot.com/2008/02/on-christian-civility.html.

2. Martin E. Marty, in Quentin J. Schultze, *Communicating for Life: Stewardship in Community and Media* (Grand Rapids MI: Baker Academic, 2000).

3. James B. Smith, "Gospel-free Sunday," *Florida Baptist Witness,* 29 May 2008.

4. Ken Connor, "Words Really Do Matter," http://townhall.com/columnists/KenConnor/2008/02/24/ words_really_do_matter, 24 February 2008.

5. Johnson Oatman, "Count Your Many Blessings," *Songs for Young People* (Chicago: Edwin O. Excell, 1897).

6. Romans 8:26 RSV.

7. Matthew 5:23 NRSV.

8. John 13:34-35 NRSV.

9. Schultze, *Communicating for Life* (Grand Rapids MI: Baker Academic, 2000) 173.

10. Robert Banks and R. Paul Stevens, *The Complete Book of Everyday Christianity* (Downers Grove IL: InterVarsity Press, 1997).

11. Wes White, http://johannesw2slianus.blogspot.com/2008/02/on-christian-civility.html.

12. Joseph Telushkin, *Words that Hurt; Words that Heal* (New York: Quill, 1996) 3.

13. Alfred, Lord Tennyson, *Alfred, Lord Tennyson: Selected Poems* (New York: Everyman's Poetry Library, 1997).

14. Psalm 19:14 AV.

15. Arthur Caliandro, *Make Your Life Count* (San Francisco: Harper & Row, 1980) 102.

16. C. Mitchell Carnell, Jr., 1996.

17. Peggy Andersen, *Great Quotes from Great Leaders* (Naperville IL: SimpleTruths, 2007) 24.

Contributors

Jimmy R. Allen

Jimmy Allen most recently served as the coordinator of the New Baptist Covenant Celebration that brought together more than thirty Baptist denominations. He is a past president of the Southern Baptist Convention and the General Baptist Convention of Texas. In 1999 he was cited as one of the ten most influential Texas Baptists of the twentieth century by the Texas *Baptist Standard*. He was the president and CEO of the Radio and Television Commission of the Southern Baptist Convention and won an Emmy for *China, Walls and Bridges*, a program filmed in China and produced by ABC News. His book *Burden of a Secret: A Story of Truth and Mercy in a Family Faced with AIDS* is a plea for churches to banish fear. In 1974 he received the Citation of Merit from the government of Honduras for humanitarian service in the wake of a natural disaster. Dr. Allen led a fact-finding mission to Iran during the hostage crisis at the United States embassy in Teheran (1979–1980). He and his wife, Linda, live in Big Canoe, Georgia.

Wade Burleson

Wade Burleson has served as pastor of Emmanuel Baptist Church in Enid, Oklahoma, since 1992. He has twice served as president of the Oklahoma Baptist Convention and also served as its parliamentarian. He was a trustee of the International Mission Board of the Southern Baptist Convention. He and his wife, Rachelle, met at Baylor University and they have four children. He graduated from East Central University in Ada, Oklahoma. He is the author of *Hardball Religion, Happiness Doesn't Just Happen*, and *The Life of John Gano*. It is his blog, *Grace and Truth to You* (www.wadeburleson.com), that thrust him onto center stage in the uses of the Internet in religious circles.

Mitch Carnell

Mitch Carnell was president and CEO of the Charleston (SC) Speech and Hearing Center for thirty-five years. He is a fellow of the American Speech Language and Hearing Association and was awarded the honors of the South Carolina Association. He was awarded South Carolina's highest citizenship award, the Order of the Palmetto. He is the author of *Development, Management and Evaluation of the Community Speech and Hearing Center, Speaking in Church Made Simple,* and *Say Something Nice; Be a Lifter.* He wrote a column for fourteen years, "Speaking Frankly," for *Business Review* published by the *Charleston* (SC) *Post and Courier.* He is the originator of Say Something Nice Day and Say Something Nice Sunday. He holds degrees from Mars Hill College, Furman University, the University of Alabama, and Louisiana State University. Carol, his wife, retired as a business education teacher from Charleston County Schools.

Sally Dyck

Sally Dyck is the resident bishop of the United Methodist Church of Minnesota. She received her ministerial training at the Boston University School of Theology, earned a World Council of Churches graduate certificate from the University of Geneva, and holds a graduate degree from Union Theological Seminary. Before going to Minnesota, she served in the East Ohio Conference as a pastor and superintendent. She served on the board of directors for the general board of Global Missions and was elected to the Central Committee of the World Council of Churches. She is a frequent conference speaker and facilitator. She is married to Kenneth Ehrman, a United Methodist Church elder.

John Gehring

John Gehring is a senior writer and media specialist for Catholics in Alliance for the Common Good. Previously he was the assistant for media relations at the U.S. Conference of Catholic Bishops, where he provided media outreach and commentary writings for the bishops and staff on international justice and peace, immigration, and other social justice issues. He was a reporter for *Education Week* and has written for the *Catholic Review* in Baltimore and the *Frederick* (MD) *Gazette.* He holds degrees from Mount St. Mary's University and Columbia University.

Alexia Kelley

Alexia Kelley is the executive director and co-founder of Catholics in Alliance for the Common Good. She worked for nearly a decade at the Catholic Campaign for Human Development. She is co-author (with Chris Korzen) of *A Nation for All: How the Catholic Vision for the Common Good Can Save America from the Politics of Division* and is co-editor of *Living the*

Catholic Social Tradition: Cases and a Commentary. She has a BA in religion with honors from Haverford and a Master of Theological Studies from Harvard Divinity School.

Thomas R. McKibbens

Thomas McKibbens has been the senior pastor of First Baptist Church of Worcester, Massachusetts, since February of 2003, following twelve years as the senior minister of First Baptist Church at Newton, Massachusetts. He has been a seminary professor for thirty years, teaching at Harvard Divinity School, Boston University School of Theology, Southeastern Baptist Theological Seminary, Southern Baptist Theological Seminary, and Andover Newton Theological School where he is also a trustee. In addition to a number of chapters and articles, McKibbens is the author of *The Forgotten Heritage: A Linage of Great Baptist Preaching* and co-author of *The Life and Work of Morgan Edwards*. He and his wife, Donna, have two grown children.

Richard J. Mouw

Richard Mouw is president of Fuller Theological Seminary. He was professor of Christian philosophy at Calvin College for seventeen years. He has also served as a visiting professor to the Free University of Amsterdam. He received his education at Houghton College, the University of Alberta, and the University of Chicago. He has written seventeen books, including *Uncommon Decency: Christian Civility in an Uncivil World*, *Calvinism in the Los Vegas Airport: Making Connections in Today's World*, and *Praying at Burger King*. He has contributed to numerous publications and is a frequent contributor to beliefnet.com. Dr. Mouw writes a blog titled "Mouw's Musings" (http://www.netbloghost.com/mouw). His wife, Phyllis, is an art historian.

Paul B. Raushenbush

Paul B. Raushenbush is the associate dean of Religious Life and the Chapel at Princeton University. Paul studied religion at Macalester College before attending Union Theological Seminary in New York City where he graduated with distinction. An ordained American Baptist minister, Rev. Raushenbush has served at Seattle First Baptist Church, the Presbyterian Chaplaincy at Columbia University, and as College and Young Adult Minister at The Riverside Church in New York City. A contributor to several journals and magazines, Dean Raushenbush is a contributing editor for Beliefnet.com and moderator of the blog *Progressive Revival*. He has been the chaplain at the Chautauqua Institute and at the College of Preachers at the National Cathedral, and he has spoken at universities around the country. His first book, *Teen Spirit: One World, Many Faiths*, was released in Fall 2004. He is the editor of the hundredth-anniversary edition of Walter Rauschenbusch's book *Christianity and the Social Crisis In the 21st Century*. Rev. Raushenbush serves as the co-director of the Program on Religion, Diplomacy and International Relations at The Liechtenstein Institute on Self Determination at Princeton University.

Stacy F. Sauls

A former lawyer, Stacy Sauls is the resident bishop of the Episcopal Diocese of Lexington, Kentucky. Before being elected bishop, he served churches in Griffin, Savannah, and Atlanta, Georgia. He received his education at Furman University, the University of Virginia School of Law, the General Theological Seminary, and Cardiff University (Wales). He serves as a member of the executive council of the Episcopal Church and the standing committee on constitution and canons. He is a member of the board of Forward Movement Publications, the Episcopal Media Center, and the American Committee for the Kiyosato Environmental Education Project in Japan. He is the author or co-author of two Forward Movement pamphlets, *That We May Evermore Dwell in Him and He in Us* and *What to Say to Your Neighbors When They Ask about the Church and Gays*, and writes a blog titled *Canterbury Tales: Reflections of an Anglican Pilgrim and Bishop* (www.kentucky.com/995). His wife, Ginger, is a special education teacher. They have two sons.

Breinigsville, PA USA
23 September 2009
224649BV00002B/4/P